CCCC STUDIES IN WRITING & RHETORIC
Edited by Victor Villanueva, Washington State University

The aim of the CCCC Studies in Writing & Rhetoric (SWR) Series is to influence how we think about language in action and especially how writing gets taught at the college level. The methods of studies vary from the critical to historical to linguistic to ethnographic, and their authors draw on work in various fields that inform composition—including rhetoric, communication, education, discourse analysis, psychology, cultural studies, and literature. Their focuses are similarly diverse—ranging from individual writers and teachers, to work on classrooms and communities and curricula, to analyses of the social, political, and material contexts of writing and its teaching.

SWR was one of the first scholarly book series to focus on the teaching of writing. It was established in 1980 by the Conference on College Composition and Communication (CCCC) in order to promote research in the emerging field of writing studies. As our field has grown, the research sponsored by SWR has continued to articulate the commitment of CCCC to supporting the work of writing teachers as reflective practitioners and intellectuals.

We are eager to identify influential work in writing and rhetoric as it emerges. We thus ask authors to send us project proposals that clearly situate their work in the field and show how they aim to redirect our ongoing conversations about writing and its teaching. Proposals should include an overview of the project, a brief annotated table of contents, and a sample chapter. They should not exceed 10,000 words.

To submit a proposal, please register as an author at www.editorialmanager.com/nctebp. Once registered, follow the steps to submit a proposal (be sure to choose SWR Book Proposal from the drop-down list of article submission types).

SWR Editorial Advisory Board

Victor Villanueva, SWR Editor, Washington State University
Anna Plemons, Associate Editor, Washington State University
Frances Condon, University of Waterloo
Ellen Cushman, Northeastern University
Deborah Holdstein, Columbia College Chicago
Asao Inoue, University of Washington Tacoma
Jay Jordan, University of Utah
Min-Zhan Lu, University of Louisville
Paula Mathieu, Boston College
Nedra Reynolds, University of Rhode Island
Jacqueline Rhodes, Michigan State University
Eileen Schell, Syracuse University
Jody Shipka, University of Maryland, Baltimore County
Vershawn Ashanti Young, University of Waterloo

INSIDE THE SUBJECT
A THEORY OF IDENTITY FOR THE STUDY OF WRITING

Raúl Sánchez
University of Florida

Conference on College Composition and Communication

National Council of Teachers of English

Staff Editor: Bonny Graham
Manuscript Editor: Lee Erwin
Series Editor: Victor Villanueva
Interior Design: Mary Rohrer
Cover Design: Mary Rohrer and Lynn Weckhorst

NCTE Stock Number: 23454; eStock Number: 23478
ISBN 978-0-8141-2345-4; eISBN 978-0-8141-2347-8

Copyright © 2017 by the Conference on College Composition and Communication of the National Council of Teachers of English.

All rights reserved. No part of this publication may be reproduced or transmitted in any form or by any means, electronic or mechanical, including photocopy, or any information storage and retrieval system, without permission from the copyright holder. Printed in the United States of America.

It is the policy of NCTE in its journals and other publications to provide a forum for the open discussion of ideas concerning the content and the teaching of English and the language arts. Publicity accorded to any particular point of view does not imply endorsement by the Executive Committee, the Board of Directors, or the membership at large, except in announcements of policy, where such endorsement is clearly specified.

NCTE provides equal employment opportunity (EEO) to all staff members and applicants for employment without regard to race, color, religion, sex, national origin, age, physical, mental or perceived handicap/disability, sexual orientation including gender identity or expression, ancestry, genetic information, marital status, military status, unfavorable discharge from military service, pregnancy, citizenship status, personal appearance, matriculation or political affiliation, or any other protected status under applicable federal, state, and local laws.

Every effort has been made to provide current URLs and email addresses, but because of the rapidly changing nature of the Web, some sites and addresses may no longer be accessible.

Library of Congress Cataloging-in-Publication Data

Names: Sánchez, Raúl, 1965- author.
Title: Inside the subject : a theory of identity for the study of writing / Raúl Sánchez.
Description: Urbana, Illinois : National Council of Teachers of English, 2017 | Series: CCCC studies in writing & rhetoric | Includes bibliographical references and index.
Identifiers: LCCN 2017015631 (print) | LCCN 2017035288 (ebook) | ISBN 9780814123478 | ISBN 9780814123454 (pbk.) | ISBN 9780814123478 (ebook)
Subjects: LCSH: Authorship. | Identity (Philosophical concept) | English language—Rhetoric. | Composition (Language arts)
Classification: LCC PN145 (ebook) | LCC PN145 .S196 2017 (print) | DDC 808.02—dc23
LC record available at https://lccn.loc.gov/2017015631

CONTENTS

Acknowledgments   vii
Introduction: Acts of Writing   1

1. The Outside of Texts   19
2. Everyday Iterability   38
3. Theories of Identity   57
4. Distributing Invention   74
5. Conclusion: Theory as Method   98

Works Cited   115
Index   123
Author   127

ACKNOWLEDGMENTS

THANKS FIRST AND FOREMOST TO MY PARTNER AND colleague, Maria Rogal, whose unfailing encouragement helped me see this project through. She is my fiercest advocate, my best friend, and the love of my life.

Thanks also to the University of Florida Department of English for providing a stimulating, inspiring, and collegial atmosphere in which to think and work. I mean my extraordinary colleagues, of course, especially those who have chaired our department since I arrived, thereby letting the rest of us do our work: John Leavey, Ira Clark, Pamela Gilbert, Kenneth Kidd, and Sid Dobrin.

But I mean also the students—undergraduate and graduate—who have endured my theoretical musings and pedagogical experiments (even when neither worked out as I had imagined), and whose writing processes continue to fascinate me.

And I mean the office professionals who, on a daily basis, have enriched and improved my working life with their skill, graciousness, and patience: Carla Blount, Melissa Davis, Kathy Williams, John Murchek, Jeri White, and Janet Moore.

Thanks as well to my friends and colleagues in the Latinx Caucus of NCTE/CCCC, who for twenty-three years have reminded me—through their work and their example—that being true to yourself is the best way to be true to your profession. Chief among these friends and colleagues, of course, is Victor Villanueva, who continues to mean so much to so many of us, but also Amanda Espinosa-Aguilar, Cristina Kirklighter, Jaime Mejía, Luisa Rodríguez Connal, Cecilia Rodríguez Milanés, Iris Ruiz, and all the "youngsters" who continue to swell our ranks every year.

Thanks in particular to Susan Miller, whose influence abides in each paragraph of this book and in every bit of my work.

Thanks to my family, who sustain me more than they probably imagine: my parents, Iris and Raul; my sisters Michelle, Suzy, Jenny, and their beautiful families; my in-laws, Colleen and Michael; my sister-in-law, Melanie; and my goddaughter, Olga Marie.

Thanks last but not at all least to Mies, the Modernist Cat; and to Apollonia, a.k.a. The Furrie Queene.

INTRODUCTION: ACTS OF WRITING

IN "TRACING PROCESS: HOW TEXTS COME INTO BEING," Paul Prior claims that despite the great care we might take to analyze and describe the various factors that inform writing, there is "no way to get the whole story of any text" (172). And yet, despite the truth of this statement, we have come to know a great deal about what writing is, how it works, and how it might be taught. The field of composition studies has developed many valuable theories and methods with which to study what Prior refers to as "the intersection of the cognitive and the social in activity that is distributed across individual acts, collaborative interactions, and many socially and historically developed tools" (197). And, more and more, we understand that to study writing is precisely to attend to such intersections and distributions, because we realize that the relation between writing and the rest of the world is, in a significant way, what defines writing itself.

Our field's attention to writing's relations has been especially acute over the last two decades or so. Russel Durst claims that by the late 1980s and early 1990s composition's attention to individual writing activity had reached a saturation point. He notes that "composing process studies had gone as far as they could go in yielding useful, illuminating pictures of writers' general approaches" and that, as a result, scholars in the field began looking at "other aspects of writing," namely, its connections to other activities, institutions, and phenomena (80–81). This book proceeds from the various relational turns that the study of writing has taken. But I am motivated by the sense that, despite Durst's claim, we may not have gone as far as possible toward describing the "individual acts" of writing to which Prior refers. In this sense, my argument coincides with that of Janis Haswell and Richard Haswell, who identify a "dark synapse" between the inputs of "society and culture" and the outputs of "text and response" that have occupied our field's theoretical, empirical, and pedagogical attention for decades (2). Likewise, my argument might be part of what Bruce McComiskey has called the "integrationist movement," an attempt by various scholars to complicate James Berlin's extraordinarily influential taxonomy of composition studies by combining various of its elements, particularly the expressivist and social-epistemic "camps" (751).

But where Haswell and Haswell approach these individual acts phenomenologically, through a focus on authoring defined as "the inward act that triggers the outward act of writing," I approach the question through what I see as the problematics inherent to writing itself. Like their book, *Authoring*, this book offers a conceptual orientation that can begin to account for individual acts that are invariably situated within networks, ecologies, and other sets of relations. Like other studies we might consider integrationist—Thomas Newkirk's *The Performance of Self in Student Writing*, Robert Yagelski's *Literacy Matters*, and Donna LeCourt's *Identity Matters* (which I discuss in Chapter 3)—this book tries to account for both the materiality and the discursivity that make up the individual writer, that function within the writing agent, so to speak. In doing so, this book calls continuing attention to writing's indispensable role in producing the very notions of interiority and exteriority that inform our understandings of writing itself, and that we map onto writers' bodies. Basically, I hope to provide a theoretical resource that helps account for the knotty difficulties of using writing to discuss the functions of writing.

In *The Function of Theory in Composition Studies*, I criticized the idea that writing is best approached as a technology of representation, on the grounds that this perspective limits our field's ability to account for the full range of writing's cultural work—its relations with other parts of the world. I argued for greater understanding of writing's relations by urging us to expand the range of interactions we can imagine between acts of writing and the world. Because of this, it might seem odd for me to now emphasize the individual act, to focus on the supposed interiority of the writer, to try to isolate a moment that is deeply integrated with and inextricably related to things around it. But writing's relationality is precisely what makes possible my attention to interiority and the individual act. In other words, it's not that I want to separate writing from its many contexts. I don't mean to argue against what is now common disciplinary knowledge: that writing is profoundly and even essentially relational. But I do intend to trace and apply the consequences of that knowledge "down" to the most discrete and empirically available level: the moment of a text's creation by a physical body. If multiple streams of discourse, data, and symbols can be said to inform an individual act of writing, and if that individual act of writing is carried out by an agent, then this book offers terms for discussing that flow as it passes "through" that agent.

On the question of interiority, Prior's distinction between "inscription" and "composing" prompts a useful bit of reflection (168). According to Prior, inscription describes the purely physical motion of "writing with pen in hand on paper or typing with keyboard on an electronic screen" while composing describes a cognitive act, such as "when a person plans a text or even drafts out language mentally or in conversation with others" (168, 169). But I think the distinction is perhaps not so firm, particularly in light of what James Britton long ago referred to as "shaping at the point of utterance" (61), which suggests a complexity inherent in the act of writing that Prior's terms ultimately may not be able to accommodate. We might say that to distinguish between inscription and composing is to reflect assumptions about writing that force us to look through rather than at it, to borrow terms from Richard Lanham (*Literacy* 58). If inscription is what happens *out there* (as marks on a page or pixels on a screen) and composition happens *in here* (in mental states that are essentially private despite multiple input streams of text and information), then we are left, once again, with a conception of writing as fundamentally a technology of representation. We may have usefully complicated the contexts in which (and from which) writing acts happen, but those individual acts remain as mysterious as ever. And they remain mysterious because our conception assumes rather than describes a dynamic between a supposed inside and a supposed outside of writing. It does not address the implicit theory that informs the empirical question, Prior's question, of "how texts come into being." In order to explore that theory, we must attend to the idea that a major part of what defines writing is its ability to function *as if* it represents something exterior to it—things, ideas, emotions, and so on—irrespective of our own thoughts about whether or how it actually represents such things. However, I am not concerned with exteriority from an ontological perspective. Instead, I am interested in the functional aspect of exteriority, which I see as the idea that every act of writing depends upon and proceeds from the notion that there is something beyond or outside of it. For composition studies, this becomes an important issue when we connect that act of writing to an individual human body, at which point the question of interiority—metaphorical and empirical—necessarily arises. I want to propose a set of terms that takes this complex relationship between exteriority and interiority into account as fully as possible when we consider the writers with whom we work every day.

THE OUTSIDE

While I prefer to avoid philosophical discourse, I must use some philosophical terminology in proposing this theory, if only to be as careful as possible about what I mean when I use terms that might carry or at least imply a philosophical dimension. I will explore this question in greater detail in Chapter 1, but for the moment I want to note that I will use the term *outside* as a synonym for exteriority. Both terms mark the idea that there are things beyond or different from symbols, and which we think of as being represented by symbols. In the old deconstructive sense, I am referring to signifieds, which are said to be represented by signifiers within the formation of the sign.

Of course, deconstruction complicated existing descriptions of the relationship between signifier and signified, making the very idea of the signified a function of signification. In other words, if "signified" is itself a signifier, what signified does it represent? Likewise, what is the outside to which *outside* refers, and how could we access it except through symbols? On the one hand, this is now a decades-old question whose answers we in composition studies have learned, perhaps even internalized depending on how much they impinge upon our own research and teaching practices. But to say that we know this question and its various answers—to say that we know the various terms (*différance,* supplementarity, the trace, and so on) that were developed to confront this question—is not to say that the question is less provocative now than when it was first articulated, or that it poses fewer challenges for the study of writing. In fact, I believe that despite our familiarity with the intricacies of symbolic action or signification, the idea of the *outside*—of exteriority—remains elusive and difficult, in part because we treat it as a philosophical rather than functional issue. I believe we inadvertently and especially treat it this way when we simply assume its existence—that is, when we take it for granted or do not see it as an important theoretical issue. In turn, this stealth philosophical perspective informs our theories and methods for studying writing. For example, it informs Prior's claim about there being "no way to get the whole story of any text." Our disciplinary ideas and our commonsense notions about writing preserve a philosophical legacy.

So it is not without a sense of irony that, by way of introduction, I turn to Jacques Derrida for an instructive meditation on the difficulties of exteriority. To me, Derrida's work has always been valuable for its relentless attention to the importance and consequences of words, terminology, and writing. But this attention has placed him at the boundary of professional philosophy itself. In fact, I tend to think of him less as a philosopher than as someone who is marginal (in the best sense of the word) to a variety of disciplines and intellectual traditions, and who derives a unique perspective precisely from being on the margins.

In "The Deaths of Roland Barthes," Derrida examines that writer's notion of the *punctum,* a term Derrida describes as referring to "a point of singularity that punctuates the surface of the reproduction—and even the production—of analogies, likenesses, and codes" (269). It is a term, according to Derrida, for "the uncoded beyond," or the outside (271). In Barthes's writing, *punctum* stands in relation to *studium*, which represents the realm of codes (or symbols, or signifiers). In reference to photography, *studium* describes for Barthes, according to Derrida, "the homogeneous objectivity of the framed space" (271). For Derrida, the idea of the *punctum* makes sense only insofar as it can be rendered in terms of the *studium*. That is, while Barthes intends the *punctum* as a way to describe the unexpected intrusion of exteriority, and while he intends it as a way to discuss moments of intensity that are outside of language, the only way it can do this is by "lend[ing] itself to metonymy" (288). In other words, "the uncoded beyond" must already be, in effect, precoded—that is, it must already be available in the symbolic forms of the *studium*.

Derrida explains that, on the one hand, "[t]he heterogeneity of the *punctum* is rigorous; its originality can bear neither contamination nor concession" (288). The experience of the *punctum* is always, by Barthes's definition, completely unique. On the other hand, it "composes with the same, with its absolute other that is thus not its opposite, with the locus of the same and of the *studium*" (288). That is, the idea of uniqueness is itself part of the code; it must be part of the code, or else we would not recognize anything as being either unique or commonplace. For Derrida, the very idea of something residing "outside all fields and all codes," the very idea of a "place of irreplaceable singularity and of the unique referential," necessarily requires "a network of substitutions" (288). So, the idea of the *outside* depends upon the work of the *inside*—the work of codes, symbols, signifiers—and vice versa. But the question for the study of writing is how to think about and describe the particulars of this interdependency. I will argue that we should see the *outside* as operational or functional rather than philosophical, metaphysical, or even given. That is, I believe that in order to understand how writing works, we should understand what role the idea of the outside plays in writing's workings. Once we do this, then we can inform our studies of writing with theories and methods that reflect our understanding.

THE OUTSIDE OF WRITING

Obviously, I think we are not there yet, which is the reason for this book. I agree with Prior, and with Haswell and Haswell, that individual acts of writing remain relatively opaque even after decades of theory and research in composition studies. I believe this is the case because acts of writing mark the very moment at which the idea of the *outside* is most relevant, and therefore most powerful. Of course, our field has a history with the *outside*, a history of working with the notion that ideas and meanings and so on come into writing from without. In 1980, when Ann Berthoff wrote that we make meanings "from the mysterious and unformed" (76), and when James Britton referred to "the moment by moment interpretative process by which we make sense of what is happening around us" (63), both were conveying a sense that the act of writing brings forth what had previously been unavailable. Their key contribution, and that of their contemporaries, was to argue for the generative role of language. But they and other voices in the process movement shared a key assumption with the current-traditional paradigm they supplanted, namely, that writing's main purpose and function was to represent. And so, the field continued—and continues—to talk about the act of writing as the bringing forth of something that had been elsewhere, outside. We still think of *the outside* as more of a realm or a place than a feature or a function.

The problem has as much to do with our terms for studying writing as it does with the complexity of writing itself. By emphasizing terminology in this book, I will also be making a claim about the role of the theorist in composition studies. While it remains important for us to offer general statements that situate research and pedagogy, and while we should develop those statements in close relationship with research and pedagogy, we should also take a step back in order to contemplate the prospect that the terms we all use to study writing are as prescriptive as they are descriptive. I am informed by Kenneth Burke's claim that "much that we take as observations about 'reality' may be but the spinning out of possibilities implicit in our particular choice of terms," and I think the consequences of this claim are significant (*Language* 46). Furthermore, I believe that the matter becomes even more difficult when we remove the element of choice. That is, while we do choose—in a very practical sense—the terms by which we study writing, we do so under historical, cultural, conceptual, rhetorical, and linguistic constraints. And even if we could choose our terms free from these constraints, we would not find terms that would not place us in a similar situation. This is because, as Burke explains, every term is part of a "nomenclature," a coherent system that "directs the attention into some channels rather than others" (*Language* 45).

THE STUDY OF WRITING

So we habitually say that writing reflects, invokes, gestures toward, or otherwise represents what is outside of it. This means we believe, or at least assume, that an act of writing is an act of indexing, which is to say that the resulting marks represent things (such as objects, ideas, etc.). This is our commonsense belief about how writing works and what it does, and it is also our disciplinary understanding of it. But I do not mean to accuse or indict the field. I think such an understanding is unavoidable, and we all share it. Nonetheless, it meets a stiff challenge in Derrida's claim that we never really "transgress the text toward something other than it, toward a referent . . . or toward a signified outside the text whose content could take place, could have taken place outside of language, that is to say . . . outside of writing in general" (*Of Grammatology* 158). In composition theory, we may agree with Derrida that the signified is perpetually elusive, that behind every instance of writing there are only ever more instances of writing. But even our ability to make and accept this claim—that it's signifiers all the way down, so to speak—depends on writing's ability to function as if this were not the case. So even when we accept a complex notion of signification, we necessarily work from a simpler one. We must assume an *outside,* even if we know or believe that the very idea of the outside is problematic.

Because of this complicated situation, it is especially important for those of us who study writing to understand and articulate how the *outside* of writing is assumed, evoked, and articulated, not just by students and writers but by theorists, researchers, and teachers in our own field. If we think of composition studies as a nomenclature about writing, we might think of our work as that of choosing key terms and their functions, and of bringing assumed terms under careful scrutiny. I want to recognize how the *outside* functions in certain key terms and concepts in our field, and I want to bring that recognition into our theoretical conversations about writing, making it the part of our nomenclature that recognizes exteriority as a function of writing, rather than that which writing tries to represent or invoke. In order to do so, I want to retheorize *identity*, a term we already use, so that it describes the relationship between the *inside* and the *outside* of writing at the moment of a text's creation—that is, during an individual act of writing.

IDENTITY'S RESOURCES

Identity is a term with some history in composition studies, but with even more history in other interdisciplinary areas, particularly cultural theory. There the term carries considerable theoretical baggage, most of it laid on by poststructuralist theory in the 1980s and 1990s. According to cultural theorist Susan Hegeman, poststructuralism attacked "some of the foundational assumptions of identity-based political movements" (67). She sees the encounter between theory and identity as having been "creative" in that it forced theorists and other proponents of identity to reexamine their notions of "subjectivity, social construction, language, and power" (68). However, she also notes that, even today, a "philosophically adequate meeting point between poststructuralist and identitarian positions" remains elusive (69). As a result, she claims, theorists of various kinds have simply dropped the question of the relationship between theory and identity: on the one hand, "there are plenty of people out there who are ready to argue that poststructuralism is a dead letter," and on the other hand, "there have always been those who felt that too much time was spent worrying over categories like race and gender" (72). Well into the twenty-first century, then, it seems that the question of identity in cultural theory is as contested as ever, and that the basic issues have remained in place since the late 1980s.

For composition studies, I think neither of these long-standing positions is useful, nor is an ongoing state of undecidability between them. For reasons I will discuss in Chapter 2, I think we cannot disregard the insights of poststructural theory on questions of identity and agency. But neither can we discard identity, precisely because we are invested—historically and pedagogically—in agents and agency. Writing's agents are, after all, our field's reason for being. Writers have been our most urgent and consistent objects of inquiry, despite significant theoretical and methodological differences in how we approach them. A writer of some sort abides, implicitly or explicitly, in most of composition's theories, research studies, and practices. Because *identity* is a term historically and conceptually connected to agents (in composition studies and elsewhere), we might arrive at some interesting and useful theoretical insights that can inform future inquiries if we can articulate identity with some of our field's other terms and concepts for studying writers. As I see it, the challenge for our field, in a sense, is to resolve what cultural theory has been unable to resolve: this impasse between the postmodern critique of identity and identity's continuing currency. Regarding poststructuralist theory, I follow a path clearly marked by such compositionists as Jasper Neel and Sharon Crowley, who see in Derrida's work a powerful set of terms for thinking about and studying writing. Furthermore, I think his work is especially valuable for contemporary scenes of writing. Regarding identity theory, I follow our field's valuing of the empirical, and our history of seeing the political dimensions of writing research and writing instruction. In so doing, I recognize that *identity* can provide the material specificity that poststructuralist theory lacks on its own. Finally, I believe identity's connection to agency makes it relevant to our field's mission to know the vicissitudes of writing so that we may help empower as many people—as many writers—as possible.

It seems clear to me, then, that *identity* can affect current conversations in the field and perhaps start new ones. These include questions about how and where an act of writing begins. Prior notes that "many accounts of writing processes bracket off the task [of inquiring about beginnings], taking it as a given" despite the fact that "all the elements of initiation and motivation—the emergence of some text as write-able in some context—are central to tracing the process" (168). If we want to know as much as possible about writing, we should know something of how it begins. I think *identity* can help us answer such questions because, when theorized a certain way, it raises fundamental questions about the relationship between the *outside* and the *inside*, which also happen to be questions about invention, as I will discuss in Chapters 4 and 5. This book is my attempt to theorize identity in this certain way.

Finally, I think there is a larger reason for reckoning with identity and bringing it more explicitly into our theories and methodologies. Regardless of what any of us might think about *identity* as a term or concept, it has enduring descriptive value outside of composition studies. According to sociologist Manuel Castells, people seek stability in an increasingly complex world: "When the world becomes too large to be controlled, social actors aim to shrink it back to their size and reach. When networks dissolve time and space, people anchor themselves in places, and recall their historic memory" (69). Castells argues that to avoid being "lost in the whirlwind of information flows and cross-organizational networks," we create identities that "provide refuge, solace, certainty, and protection" (69, 70). These identities are narratives about who we are, where we come from, and what we believe in. According to Castells, "the (re)construction of meaning by defensive identities breaks away from the institutions of society, and promises to rebuild from the bottom up" (70). This process "may be the main potential source of social change in the network society," though this is not "an historical necessity," and its outcomes—positive or negative—are far from certain (70). But if Castells is right, then it seems undeniable that in increasingly deterritorialized information and material environments, people will keep searching for ways to define themselves socially, culturally, politically, and individually. And they will do this by making texts of all kinds. They will do this by writing.

THE EVENT

Another term for describing the relation between the *outside* and *inside* of writing is the event. In certain strands of contemporary theory, it is a term for describing the emergence of novelty. Alain Badiou refers to the event as that "which brings to pass 'something other' than the situation, opinions, instituted knowledges" that obtain (*Ethics* 67). Bill Readings calls it a "radically singular happening which cannot be represented within a general history without the loss of its singularity" (57). Phillip Wegner defines it as "the inauguration of that which was unexpected, unknown, and uncounted" (23). And according to Gilles Deleuze, an event is that which establishes a "line-frontier between things and propositions" (*Logic* 209). If we grant that things exist outside or independent of the representations of them that we receive and produce, then events are occasions when these things first appear. Not surprisingly, part of the event's enduring interest to theory—when conceived in this way—is its paradoxical quality. For example, if there are things (objects, ideas, situations) outside and independent of their representation in symbol systems, how can we know about them before they become represented? After all, terms such as *object, idea,* and *situation* are already representations. A disconnect between the idea of the event and the idea of representation (or, more precisely, the iterability that makes up representation) sits at the heart of poststructural theory and its critique of philosophical discourse.

But I am concerned with issues that brush up against philosophy only to the extent that they help shed light on writing. The idea of something called *the event* is interesting to me because, like identity, it speaks to the idea of beginnings, and to the idea of novelty's emergence. As a result, it can help describe what happens at Britton's "point of utterance," at the part of writing that Prior correctly claims we take for granted. In fact, every act of writing is *evental.* If a text is a representation, or a series of representations, then we might describe its making as evental insofar as we suppose these representations stand in for things. In this sense, the act of writing materializes Deleuze's "line-frontier." More important, to say that acts of writing are events is to define theoretically what every teacher knows from practice: that to write is to do something more complex and complicated than simply representing the *outside* on the *inside*.

My specific theoretical goal, then, is to use *identity* as *event* to refine our field's ways of thinking about what is happening when individuals write. Like most people in our field, I work from the assumption that acts of writing are irreducibly complex. Furthermore, I believe that this complexity cannot be usefully "boiled down" for purposes of research, pedagogy, or more theory. On the contrary, our terms and concepts for studying writing should be rich and flexible enough to shed light on this complexity in productive ways.

The first chapter examines in detail the issue of exteriority, or the *outside*. Specifically, I propose exteriority as a constitutive feature of writing, one that postmodern theory treats with insufficient seriousness—or at least not with the kind of seriousness that composition studies requires due to its abiding concern with writing's agents. I argue that because exteriority is built into writing (and any other kind of symbol system), the essentialism that postmodern theory rejects is inevitable and unavoidable. Because exteriority is built into writing and because our field attends to writing's agents, I argue that composition studies is not and never has been in a position to either accept or reject the idea of empiricism. Furthermore, many of our field's past debates about the value and uses of empiricism have since been obviated by new scenes and technologies of writing. We can now pool previous methodological and ideological differences, intermingling and applying them to the core question of what happens when a text is made by an agent. And this intermingling can take place within the framework of identity.

Toward this end, I examine two perspectives that recognize and try to work through the apparent impasse generated by, on the one hand, postmodern critiques of identity and, on the other hand, the exigencies of materiality that seem to endure despite these critiques. First, I examine Mark Hansen's and N. Katherine Hayles's attempts to theorize technology and bodies—two ostensible components of exteriority—in light of postmodern theory. Then, I look at Satya Mohanty's and Linda Martin Alcoff's efforts to establish a viable theory of identity in light of the many antiessentialist critiques of that concept. Each of these perspectives sheds light on the question of exteriority, and each offers ways to think about it seriously without rejecting postmodern theories.

In the context of composition studies, to take exteriority seriously is to recognize that it gives voice to the idea that acts of agency—including acts of writing—start. It is to acknowledge the persistence of origin stories within discourse itself, as part of discourse's very mechanism. In treating exteriority this way, I establish the exigency on which the rest of the book is based: the need for composition studies to develop an approach—apart from specific theories, research methodologies, and pedagogies—to writing's agents in technologized scenes of contemporary writing, scenes that increasingly distribute, attenuate, or otherwise diminish the role of agents. My goal is not only to "rescue the subject" but to underscore that subject's inevitability and to provide an appropriate vocabulary for describing that inevitability.

The second chapter asks what it means to say that individuals write—that they exercise agency—in contexts of networked subjectivity and distributed agency. I examine key theories of rhetoric and writing for contemporary technological spaces and environments. I explore consequences of the idea that writing serves purposes other than to communicate messages or represent information. I examine the viability of imagining writing as the context in which such notions as *communication* and *representation* become intelligible in the first place. In the context of contemporary technology, writing's iterability becomes ever more prominent, and this prominence in turn raises questions about writing acts and writing's agents. Specifically, to what extent does it make sense to see an act of writing as a collage of previously available symbols and ideas governed by the strict conventionality of words, sounds, and images? Following Haswell and Haswell, might we instead imagine that every act of writing contains or enacts something irreducible and singular, an event that intrudes, erupts, or emerges into representation and therefore into the conventions that define writing as a technology? This irreducibility is not something that a concept such as iterability can accommodate, at least not to the extent required by our field.

What I mean is that iterability alone does not account for—was never meant to account for—the moment of inscription, the point of written utterance. It must be supplemented with a theory of the event. And here is where identity, understood in terms of the event, can contribute to theoretical perspectives on writing acts: we can use identity to mark exteriority's necessary role in producing—not just distributing—texts. Similarly to that of exteriority, the status of identity as a feature of writing gives us a way into a discourse that is otherwise indifferent or even hostile to the question of production: the question of what is involved when a text is made.

The third chapter articulates this event-based theory of identity. I begin with an overview of the problems that have attended to the concept of identity outside the field since the 1980s and 1990s. I explain as well some of the uses to which identity has been put during this time. In acknowledging identity's turbulent history in cultural studies and critical theory, I hope to underscore the fact that its political and pedagogical usefulness, its theoretical difficulty, and the various discussions about its usefulness and difficulty *all* indicate how central it should be to any discussion of writing's agents in contexts that contemporary technologies have affected profoundly. Even though over time there may not have been widespread agreement about the role or value of identity as a concept, the very fact that it resurfaces in discussions about agency suggests that it speaks to a sense that there ought to be something else outside of or beyond textuality, discursivity, or symbolic action. For my purposes, then, identity is not something to be for or against. Rather, it names a necessary function of writing.

This chapter examines how identity has been used within composition studies as well. I focus on the difference between *identity* and *identities*, showing how scholars' use of one or the other—or both—tells us something about their theoretical orientation. In composition studies, *identity* usually refers to a theoretical concept, while *identities* indicates a lived experience. The difference between these is not absolute, and of course the terms are related, but when we conflate them we create certain conceptual problems that manifest themselves at levels of theory, research, and ultimately pedagogy. After raising this theoretical or methodological caution, I turn to recent work in composition studies that tackles the concept of identity directly.

If our field's concern with writing's agents necessarily leads to questions about how writing begins, then the search for such beginnings necessarily leads back to questions about exteriority—that is, about the notion that something comes from *the outside* at the moment of inscription, at the point of written utterance. By focusing on Donna LeCourt's *Identity Matters,* I look at how theories of identity as performative have been brought to bear on this question. The main issue, in LeCourt's book and elsewhere, is one that we might expect in composition studies: a question of how materiality intersects with the textuality or discursivity that student writers necessarily inhabit, mainly through academic discourse. LeCourt borrows Stuart Hall's concept of *suture* to discuss this intersection, and she urges the field to pay more careful attention to the impacts and consequences of embodiment on the writing lives of students. In effect, she sees the student body as one precise location of suture, and asks composition studies to take this into account as it exercises its prevailing performative notions of identity. LeCourt's study helpfully articulates one aspect of the theoretical question I am trying to address: as it tries to shed light on how texts begin, how should an agent-oriented field such as composition studies articulate the idea of exteriority in contexts of technologized and textualized postmodernity?

If LeCourt points to this question, Dana Anderson's *Identity's Strategy* tries to answer it, at least with regard to rhetorical theory, and so I turn to it next. Anderson tries to extend the performative theory of identity often associated with postmodern theories by arguing, via Kenneth Burke, that any human activity (performative or otherwise) is dialectical at its core because it involves the use of symbols. In this sense, identity is indeed "performed," but the performance is implicit in language itself rather than in the conscious intention or even the unconscious motivation of any particular agent. Of course, Judith Butler's performative theory of identity acknowledges the central role of language, particularly in its reference to "the grammatical time of the subject" (*Psychic* 117), but Anderson's framework is explicitly rhetorical, and explicitly concerned with rhetorical theory. This means that, to a certain extent, its approach to exteriority is less encumbered by philosophical concerns than it might otherwise be. In the end, I believe we do not need to accept or deny anything in particular about this exteriority, not even, philosophically speaking, its existence. All we need is a nomenclature that lets us talk about the fact that it seems to endure, that it seems to be a built-in feature of symbol use itself.

For such a nomenclature, this chapter returns to the question of the *event*. Despite extensive writing on the subject by philosophers, I focus on Derrida's discussion in a posthumously published essay. Again, his scrupulous attention to terms and to writing situates his discourse rather differently than that of more widely acknowledged theorists of the event, such as Badiou and Deleuze. In their writing (particularly Badiou's), one identifies a very philosophical desire to get past the problem of language, while for Derrida seeing language as a problem is the mistake philosophy has been making for centuries. Consequently, Derrida's perspective on *event* casts the relationship between exteriority and textuality in terms that we might call rhetorical (though he does not use that word) rather than philosophical.

The fourth chapter brings event-based identity to bear upon contemporary theories of invention, extending the ecological sensibilities of these theories to the point of utterance itself. Contemporary theories of invention offer sophisticated conceptual accounts of the contemporary scenes of writing, especially those mediated so thoroughly by networked technologies. They theorize invention via metaphors of intricacy and relation such as genre, complexity, ambience, and the interface. As a result, our field's image of the scene of writing is more detailed than ever before, allowing us to see invention as a distributed property rather than as the work of a singular, intentional agent. But singular agents remain a part of the landscape, even if we no longer give them ontological or epistemological pride of place. And while we can now discuss in greater conceptual detail their interactions with other parts of writing's scene, their interior functions remain, in Haswell and Haswell's words, "a remarkably black box" (2). I use this book's event-based theory of identity to illuminate that black box, as it were, by providing a terminology for talking about the boundary between exteriority and textuality as it occurs "within" the writing subject.

The fifth chapter performs a similar action with the canon of style, though it argues that style is perhaps better equipped to accommodate the question of interiority in a nonphilosophical way. I begin by looking at recent theories of style, which reflect a general dissatisfaction with what they see as that canon's history of excessive formalism and textualism, and which try to arrive at relational, contextual, and performative approaches to style that are more in keeping with contemporary scenes of writing. I examine as well the most detailed recent study of this canon, Paul Butler's *Out of Style,* focusing on its argument for a more "inventional" approach to the canon that will establish its standing as a viable avenue for the study and teaching of writing. In addressing Butler's text, I question whether it is necessary to peg style's fortunes so closely to invention in order to achieve the status Butler desires. On the one hand, mimicking invention is intellectually appealing and politically sensible. After all, invention is associated with concepts our field values, such as ideas and novelty. On the other hand, style has its own resources—resources of the surface, as it were, rather than the depths—that actually might shed different light than invention on the questions of interiority that I will have been examining in the previous chapters. Furthermore, invention itself is not what it used to be. The fourth chapter will have suggested as much, but in this chapter I turn to John Muckelbauer's *Future of Invention* to show how this canon can be usefully transformed into an ongoing theoretical problem, and to indicate the consequences of this change for the study of writing. Muckelbauer is concerned with rhetoric more than with writing, so I turn his argument more directly toward writing in order to show how the issues he raises are reflected in the questions of interiority that I will have tried to elaborate through an event-based theory of identity that can be of use to composition studies.

1

The Outside of Texts

AT THE END OF A 1989 ARTICLE IN *JAC,* Carol Berkenkotter accused some of her "hermeneutically trained colleagues" of "epistemological ethnocentricity" (79). She meant that theory-oriented scholars in composition studies mischaracterized, misunderstood, and marginalized the field's empirical research traditions. Berkenkotter's was a response of sorts to separate *JAC* articles by David Foster and John Schilb. Schilb's article, an ideological analysis of a study Berkenkotter had coauthored and published in *Research in the Teaching of English,* had stated in its conclusion that "people interested in examining the ideologies of composition and people interested in empirical research aren't reading each other's work." And it had claimed that "these factions within composition studies" were "engaged in a struggle for power" ("Ideology and" 28). Then, in 1990, responding to Berkenkotter's response, Schilb offered another analysis in which he argued that her notion of "epistemological ecumenicalism" ignored rather than addressed the question of ideology he had originally raised ("The Ideology of" 154).

I bring up this decades-old exchange because it describes a difference within composition studies that I believe exists to this day. But where Berkenkotter considered it epistemological and Schilb ideological, I think it makes as much sense to see the difference as terminological. I suggest this alternative perspective not to downplay the significance of the difference but to recast it along lines that might be more productive for the contemporary study of writing.

The original version of this chapter was previously published as "Outside the Text: Retheorizing Empiricism and Identity" in *College English* 74.3 (January 2012): 334–46. Used by permission.

With this goal in mind, I want to ask a basic question: what does composition studies study? Beginning with Janet Emig's *The Composing Processes of Twelfth Graders,* it has studied people who write, usually students. It has studied how they write, observing their writing processes as directly as possible and examining the texts they produce. Implicitly and explicitly, its goal has been to understand what is going on at that moment when people put pencil to paper, fingers to keyboard, and so on. It has tried to understand the act of writing, which we can define as the use of a common code to make an artifact that others can recognize and usually decode. Over four decades, composition studies has modified, called into question, and even criticized these goals and the assumptions behind them, particularly as it has learned more about writing's complexity. Specifically, composition theory has developed a broader and deeper notion of textuality: what Susan Miller some time ago called the "textual world" (*Rescuing* 11), a variant of what Derrida even earlier had called the "general field of writing" ("Signature" 311). In turn, this more expansive concept of textuality has allowed the field to explore the consequences of the idea that texts are situated in relation to other texts and to other parts of the world in various overarching and overlapping contexts.

But the field has done this exploring in different ways, particularly with regard to its abiding interest in writing's agents. And these ways break down just as highlighted in Berkenkotter and Schilb's exchange. On the one hand, composition's theorists—those whom Berkenkotter referred to as "hermeneutically trained"—have tended to speak of agents by referring to *the subject*. This has been a term with which to conjure theoretically, as indicated, for example, by the titles and contents of such important books as Miller's *Rescuing the Subject,* Lester Faigley's *Fragments of Rationality: Postmodernity and the Subject of Composition,* and Thomas Rickert's *Acts of Enjoyment: Rhetoric, Žižek, and the Return of the Subject.* As a term, *the subject* invokes anti- or at least non-Cartesian theoretical orientations that complicate relationships among subjects and objects, placing them all within fields of discourse. On the other hand, the field's founding term for writing's agent, *the writer,* has offered materiality. It has given empirical researchers an identifiable object of inquiry, and it has given classroom teachers an equally identifiable focal point for pedagogy. In the early to middle nineties, composition theory's emphasis on the figure of the subject yielded studies that seemed to make sense of writing's complex and intricate work in the world. But within composition's various empirical and pedagogical traditions, where the student's body necessarily figures so prominently, *the subject* did not do such work. In short, *the subject* and *the writer* were not and have not been interchangeable. And in the field as a whole, *the writer* has circulated more widely. In part this is because, as Faigley has claimed, composition studies "has remained in many respects a modernist discipline" (*Fragments* xi). In such a discipline, writing's agents are certainly implicated in complex textual relations, but at the end of the day, they exist apart from textuality. So *the subject* remains a term with which to theorize systemically, while *the writer* more aptly describes our material and individual encounters with writing's agents. Without something like *the writer's* materiality, *the subject* may continue to exert conceptual force in "hermeneutically" oriented theory, but not far beyond.

Lately, however, the conceptual gap between *the subject* and *the writer* is beginning to disappear as our understandings of writing's agents undergo significant changes as a result, in part, of recent and emerging technologies. These terms are now pointing to something more similar than they had been. For some time, theories of the subject have argued that agents, texts, and contexts are interconnected, and that they are all participants in thoroughgoing textuality. But textuality has a materiality of sorts, thanks to network and "new media" technologies. As compositionists, we're acutely aware that textuality is something people—particularly students—inhabit every day, which makes it something more than an interesting and illuminating theoretical concept. Yet, ironically, despite this awareness (or, perhaps, this meta-awareness), the experience of this thoroughgoing textuality is becoming transparent, or at least mundane. Few marvel anymore at the idea that texts travel around the world in almost no time, and we take it for granted that these kinds of texts intertwine significantly with our everyday lives through such avenues as work, leisure, activism, and finance. As I see it, this apparent transparency indicates that the terms we now have available for talking about writing agents are terms that place those agents squarely within textuality rather than apart from it. Risking glibness, I might quip that technology has caught up with theory. At the very least, it seems that the discourses of *the subject*, which had been abstract (if also insightful and provocative), might now be more material, more *writerly*, and therefore applicable to certain kinds of empirical research and to pedagogical practice. If so, then we can think about and study these contemporary experiences of textuality, which are experiences of writing, in terms of composition studies' historical concern for *the writer*. That is, if *the subject* appears to be more embodied now, we can join it to *the writer* and thus propose a new term—a new figure—for studying writing's agents. Placed at the center of composition studies, this new figure would represent and promote, simultaneously, discussions about the complex and fluid relationship between agency and textuality. Specifically, it would let us take up two previously disparate ideas and begin to think of them as conjoined and interdependent. These ideas are, first, that an act of writing can be understood as something other than the bringing forth of a pretextual intention, and second, that in order to remain a viable concept, writing as such depends precisely upon the idea of a pretextual intention. In taking them up, we might have to take on new terms; we would need a nomenclature able to walk both sides of the disappearing yet still irreducible line between the materiality of *the writer* and the discursivity of *the subject*. As I indicated in the introduction, I believe *identity* can do this work. Specifically, *identity*, theorized in terms of the concept of *the event*, offers a way to talk and think about the idea of a relation between textuality and the *outside* of textuality in a way that accounts for the field's longstanding concern with writing's agents. In this chapter, I examine *the outside*, the idea of a space or realm existing apart from textuality, but which textuality and other forms of symbolic action are said to represent.

PAST POSTMODERNISM, TOWARD A NEWER EMPIRICISM

However, in addressing the question of exteriority, of *the outside*, I am not arguing for yet another postmodern or poststructural perspective on writing and writing's agents. As valuable as I think such perspectives have been for thinking about writing, they in fact do not offer sustainable ways for composition studies to address exteriority and writing while maintaining its focus on agents. That is, they are insufficiently theoretical for our field's purposes insofar as they take textuality to be the outcome of inquiry into agency rather than its starting point. To the extent that they make a fetish of representation, they see interest in exteriority as perhaps naïve, a project unaware of its own essential discursiveness and therefore incapable of supporting knowledge claims. Or, to put it another way, we might say that postmodern orientations address the question of *the outside* from a philosophical rather than rhetorical or terminological angle.

A similar thing happened in composition studies. In the late 1980s and early 1990s, empiricism became a suspect enterprise to composition theorists who embraced postmodernism in one form or another. Scholars such as Faigley had identified composition studies as "a modernist discipline, especially in its prevailing conceptions of the subject" (xi). Others, most notably James Berlin in his 1988 *College English* article, "Rhetoric and Ideology in the Writing Class," pointed to problematic epistemological and ideological assumptions in some of the field's most influential empirical studies. Today, I think we can see that these kinds of claims ranged from being true but of unclear consequence (Faigley) to being oversimplified and overstated (Berlin). Moreover, we are well past the moment in which a larger struggle between modernism and postmodernism makes much sense, theoretically or otherwise. It is uncontroversial to point out that modernist notions played a major role in *the writer's* emergence as composition's founding figure. And I think it is equally uncontroversial to note that this legacy still offers useful and necessary terms with which to do certain kinds of work in our field. Postmodernism offered similarly helpful terms, too—the irreducibility of the signifier, Jean Baudrillard's precession of simulacra, Jean-François Lyotard's distrust of *grands récits*, and so on—with which to think about the larger contexts of writing. But now, neither of these legacies alone offers enough equipment with which to theorize, examine, and teach writing in contemporary contexts. We need more, and different, theory.

Composition theory's inability or unwillingness to reimagine empiricism back in the 1980s and 1990s might explain why some of the resistance to postmodern perspectives in the field was informed by something more than epistemological or ideological naïveté. There was a certain "common sense" behind the idea that the objects in the world can be perceived and described. After all, the very idea of a difference or a relationship between things and the symbols for things results from the fact that symbols exist: symbols are things. In this very basic sense, regardless of whether one adopts or avoids empiricism in order to study writing, empiricism abides. We are all empiricists, whether we like it or not. With this in mind, my goal is not to evaluate any particular version of empiricism but to acknowledge the empirical in this functional way, apart from the demands of any particular theory or methodology. Empiricism in this sense is less a philosophy, methodology, or ideology than an attribute, and the field—including its theorists—should approach it as such.

Specifically, we might reimagine empiricism as simultaneously a producer and a recipient of theoretical insight. But this reimagining would require more than Berkenkotter's hoped-for "epistemological ecumenicalism" of the 1980s and 1990s (79). Instead, it would require a commitment to something like Bruno Latour's claim that "[w]e don't have a very good description of anything" because we underestimate the inherent and deep complexity of objects and we mischaracterize their relationships to other objects, including the interpretive frameworks we impose upon them when we claim to merely observe them (*Reassembling* 146). To avoid these pitfalls, we would have to avoid familiar theoretical and methodological gestures such as positioning ourselves, via a framework, in relation to some object or set of objects. Instead, we would constantly articulate and rearticulate *relations* between and among the various components (including ourselves and our frameworks) in constantly proliferating and changing systems. According to Latour, these components "make everything, including their own frames, their own theories, their own contexts, their own metaphysics, even their own ontologies," and it would be the task of a new empiricism to never stop writing them up as thoroughly as possible, recognizing every framework or interpretation as itself a part of the system being described rather than a privileged perspective onto that system (147).

With such a reimagining of empiricism, we might find an array of new and useful things to say about the act of writing in contemporary contexts, though these new and useful things would not look entirely alien. That is, there are precedents for an approach similar to this in composition's own literature: Linda Flower's effort to cast qualitative empirical research in the mode of argumentation, which resulted in the notion of "observation-based theory building" (163), and Susan Miller's *Assuming the Positions,* which demonstrated that one can combine a thoroughly postmodern orientation and a broadly empirical sensibility in order to arrive at nuanced explanations of the relationships between the (re)production of texts and the (re)production of culture. Although neither of these addresses the contemporary scenes of writing, each nonetheless tries to theorize empiricism differently. And, most important, each sees empiricism as an unavoidable part of theoretical inquiry, not as an obstacle to it, and not as an option.

There are other disciplinary and historical reasons for reimagining empiricism. If we think of empiricism in its most basic sense as *looking at things in a systematic way and then making statements about them,* then we can risk banality and say that even the most resolutely "hermeneutic" work in English studies is empirical. Looking at texts—graphic, filmic, electronic, or otherwise—in systematic ways and making statements about them is the activity that connects composition studies and the rest of English studies. In this sense, again, resisting the idea of empiricism is beside the point, since everyone is already an empiricist of sorts anyway. But these concerns are ultimately secondary to the more basic issue: as it tries to describe and explain the flows and circulations of writing, composition studies needs ways to account for agency that are adequate to writing's current complexity. Specifically, it needs theory that is rigorous without being "merely" theoretical.

Composition studies will never lack research questions; we will never exhaust the topics related to the study and teaching of writing. But how we do this work—the kinds of questions we ask, the particular objects we choose to analyze—is a perpetual issue that will require our continual reevaluation. This is one of theory's tasks, and it seems especially important now, in a time of proliferating and continuously emerging technologies for making, assembling, and distributing texts of all kinds. More than ever, the study of writing needs a working and timely account of how texts come to be, of which a crucial component would be a newly theorized writing subject. This account would help to explain how specific writing subjects and specific texts interact in specific contemporary contexts. To do so, this theory would draw upon postmodernism and empiricism, taking into account that they address certain issues that still obtain. But equally, this theory would understand that what Gregory Ulmer calls "changes in the language apparatus of civilization" have taken place, and that these changes might force us to revise our conceptual and terminological apparatus (*Electronic* x).

But while we still might need the full range of available equipment, we should use it with some historical awareness. We should remember Kenneth Burke's claim that any set of terms for describing ideas, phenomena, and actions is at best creative shorthand, a form of what he calls "entitlement" rather than a faithful presentation of the real (*Language* 359). With this caveat in mind, we can still draw from empiricism and postmodernism to form part of the outline for a new approach to the study of writing. We can develop an approach to theory that historicizes, maps, and incorporates various versions of empiricism and postmodernism as needed. Informed by this approach, we might set conditions with which to examine contemporary scenes of writing. In these scenes, it may become necessary to identify a writing subject, but the challenge will be to do so without reverting to composition's default figure of the autonomous *writer,* and without hypostasizing this agent in composition theory's preferred figure of *the subject.* As Sharon Crowley notes, the field's modernist orientation allows it to cling to the notion of "a sovereign, controlling disembodied and individual voice that deploys language in order to effect some predetermined change in an audience" while its postmodern inclination claims that "individuals are neither devoid of embodiment nor free of the linguistic/cultural contexts in which they circulate" ("Body" 177). Since, as she notes, neither perspective fully confronts the question of embodiment, each is inadequate to the task at hand (178). But since their equipment remains, and since it remains influential, we will have to work with and through it to reach a new orientation toward the study of writing.

To some, it might seem that my reimagining of empiricism is an update of Gayatri Spivak's "strategic essentialism" from 1980s postcolonial theory. But I think that the present historical moment, marked as it is with technologies that "embody" the subject, calls for something more contemporary than that. It calls for theory less invested in hermeneutics and the politics of representation, more concerned with writing as a material or apparently material act. As I understand it, strategic essentialism saw the difference between the modern and the postmodern as being epistemological. At the time, doing so may have made sense. But as I mentioned above, in the current context this difference is mainly of historical interest. Furthermore, such an "unreconstructed" strategic essentialism would encourage composition theorists to do what we have often done in the past: adopt and apply existing theory rather than make a new one of our own, suited to our own disciplinary purposes. We should approach and use terms such as *modern* and *postmodern* as markers of historical and rhetorical difference. We inherit this terminology, and we should always try to be clear about its consequences for our disciplinary concerns. In the case of modernism and postmodernism, we should be careful not to assume they are simply perspectives or lenses by which to approach the world (or the text). We should see them as features, rather than descriptors, of a discursive system of which essentialism is also a part. From this perspective, *essentialism* is not an option, neither as strategy nor as tactic. Like *empiricism,* it is built in and therefore performs a function. Because we study writing, it makes more sense for us to see essentialism in this way, rather than as the result of individual or even distributed intention. In this sense, *essentialism* points us to *the outside.*

THE OUTSIDE OF POSTHUMANISM

If, like essentialism, exteriority is built in and functional, then the problem becomes how to discuss and describe it without falling into a philosophical discourse that treats it differently, as a problem of representation or even ontology. For clues, we might look at theories of technology and embodiment. These have been efforts to account for materiality of one kind or another as they relate to representation, but without reducing them to effects or results of representation. In this sense, they are attempts to come to terms with exteriority, and they resonate with the perspective I am trying to establish for the study of writing. Of course, our fields' interests and purposes are very different, especially regarding the question of agents. It is one thing to make claims about reality and the roles of writing, technology, and representation within that general reality; but it is another thing to make claims about writing and the roles of reality, technology, and representation within the general field of writing. The latter is closer to my own interests, and closer to what I think the work of our field should be. Still, these two perspectives are closely related, and they overlap somewhat. From a theoretical and methodological perspective, then, we should recognize their relationship. Yet, we should also always keep in mind the crucial differences between them, because they reflect longstanding and consequential differences between philosophy and rhetoric.

But for the moment, we can focus on similarities. For example, Mark Hansen's *Embodying Technesis: Technology beyond Writing* sees modernism and postmodernism as closely related and equally problematic in that they approach technology reductively. According to Hansen, modernism sees technology in strictly mechanical terms, while postmodernism finds it to be ultimately discursive. He is particularly concerned with postmodernism's reduction, accusing critical theory from Martin Heidegger to N. Katherine Hayles of reducing technology to a metaphor, an effect of language. And he notes that within this reduction to discourse, the language of tools and skills continues to dominate, just as it does in modernist approaches. In response, Hansen argues for an understanding of technology that fully acknowledges and takes into account its "irreducible concreteness," its effect on human beings quite apart from their ability to represent it discursively (2). He asserts an "extracultural, extrasocial dimension of technological change" that renders technologies "simply more basic than other social phenomena" (3). Because they function outside and prior to the social, "their impact on experience is at once so primitive and so pervasive that any effort to fathom it through cultural critique will have already presupposed what it sets out to isolate and identify" (3). As Hansen sees it, contemporary cultural (postmodern) criticism analyzes technology "insofar, and only insofar, as it impacts representation" in order to "overcome the difficulties involved in delimiting technology's ubiquitous and subthematic impact" (4). But because "technologies structure our lifeworlds and influence our embodied lives at a level, as it were, below the 'threshold' of representation itself," such analysis "cannot but compromise the richness and multidimensionality of technology's impact on our experience" (4).

In short, Hansen asserts what he refers to as "the robust *materiality* of technology" and in doing so asserts as well the robust materiality of the body (4). Furthermore, his theory severely restricts the power of representation. These ideas make Hansen's argument attractive and instructive, especially if we consider representation's influential and perhaps axiomatic status in composition theory. And because I would ask the field to approach acts of writing—and, in particular, moments of inscription—systemically, I am drawn toward any theory that asks us to take materiality seriously, and to do so on materiality's own terms, because I see *materiality* as an integral feature of the system. When rigorously theorized as being separate from representation, as it is in Hansen's book, it becomes yet another and possibly useful term for the *outside*.

But a great deal hinges on whether *materiality* functions as an ultimate term or a dialectical term. According to Burke, ultimate terms (or god-terms) stand at the end of "a *hierarchy*, or *sequence*, or *evaluative series*" of ideas, while dialectical terms engage "in a jangling relation with one another" (*Rhetoric* 187). Ultimate terms represent the "conclusion of dialectic" while dialectical terms function "on the level of parliamentary conflict, leading to compromise" (*Rhetoric* 276, 186–87). Because, for Burke, language itself is "essentially a means of transcending brute objects," it therefore contains within it the tendency to rank, to evaluate, even "to come upon an idea of 'God' as the ultimate transcendence" (276).

For Burke, every instance of language hints at the "conclusion of dialectic" because of this built-in "transcending" function (276). If this is the case, then we can analyze an argument such as Hansen's by identifying its ultimate terms and converting them into dialectical ones in order to map the argument relative to other, similar, ones. *Embodying Technesis* is an argument for acknowledging the *outside* of language, specifically as it relates to technology and the body. Yet one of its oft-repeated terms, *robust materiality*, simply assumes the *outside*. In this sense, it functions more like an ultimate term; it represents a concept or value that serves as a linchpin, one that we cannot question without destabilizing the hierarchy of terms leading up to it, and without questioning the basis of Hansen's argument. Hansen uses the term throughout *Embodying Technesis* to indicate something like materiality-as-such or materiality-beyond-representation. And since the entire book is an argument for materiality-as-such, the assumption and repeated assertion of *robust materiality* seems to beg the question. But in fact *robust materiality* can be as dialectical as any other term; in fact, it is as dialectical as *every* other term. The question is whether we want to accept the conditions of Hansen's argument. I think we can accept some but not others.

One thing composition studies should hesitate to accept is Hansen's key assumption about language. Hanson equates language—

and, more important, writing—with representation. Hansen hopes to "situate technology beyond writing" in order to "encompass the unthematizable contingency of technology's diffuse material impact on culture" (26). He assumes that to be "within" writing is necessarily to be within representation. From this perspective, writing is a technology of representation, a tool available for manipulation by a conscious agent, a skill without its own systemic or "material" dimension, having no particularly profound effect on being.

However, we can accept *materiality* as an important synonym for exteriority or *the outside* if it can name a function of writing rather than a feature of the world. When we approach it in this way, we acknowledge the importance of exteriority as a part of writing's work. We affirm that writing is what makes such terms as "the world" thinkable and expressible in the first place. We reject as philosophical the idea of a relationship between things and symbols. I think this stance is necessary because the philosophical framework inhabits not only most theoretical discourse but everyday language use as well. That is, the notion that the *outside* and *inside* are substantive categories that are fundamentally separate—even when imagined in an intricate relation with each other—dominates almost every aspect of the Western cultures we inhabit. And, as I noted above, I believe that debating this question is neither compelling nor relevant to composition studies. However, the notion's hegemony does require countermethodologies, ways of discussing exteriority that neither reject nor accept philosophical concerns but simply see them as separate. Of course, if Burke is right and hierarchy is implicit in language, then when I raise the question of countermethodologies, I risk lapsing (or I have already lapsed) into the same philosophical discourse I am trying to avoid. In that case, the term *counter-* names yet another feature of writing.

If *Beyond Technesis* urges us to acknowledge the *outside,* N. Katherine Hayles's *How We Became Posthuman* traces a more intricate relation between the *outside* (described as embodiment, or materiality) and the *inside* (described as textuality). Instead of strictly separating them, Hayles proposes a complex relationship between materiality and textuality by developing (and borrowing from other theorists) new terms of analysis. Like Hansen, she criticizes postmodernism's obsession with discursivity, identifying as "postmodern orthodoxy" the idea "that the body is primarily, if not entirely, a linguistic and discursive construction" (192). For Hayles, this dematerialization coincides with "cybernetic developments that stripped information of its body" in informatics and computer science (192). And she takes both as "evidence not that the body has disappeared but that a certain kind of subjectivity has emerged" (193). This subjectivity is more like a fantasy of dematerialization than its actual realization. Furthermore, it "depends in complex and highly specific ways on the *embodied* circumstances that an ideology of dematerialization would obscure" (193). What we need, according to Hayles, is "a way of talking about the body as responsive to its construction as discourse/information and yet not trapped within it," or, in other words, "a new, more flexible framework in which to think about embodiment in an age of virtuality" (193). In a way, Hayles is addressing an ongoing methodological tension in all humanistic theoretical discourse: she is trying to acknowledge the crucial, formative role of the local and the temporal while also doing the basic work of theory, which is to make general or "timeless" statements.

After an incisive critique of Foucault's "absorption of embodiment into discourse," Hayles offers a different conception of embodiment (195). She turns to Elizabeth Grosz's claim that bodies "can be represented or understood not as entities in themselves or simply on a linear continuum with its polar extremes occupied by male and female bodies . . . but as a field, a two-dimensional continuum in which race (and possibly even class, caste, or religion) form body specifications" (19). Hayles sees this field as "an interplay between two intersecting axes," whereby "the polarities defining the end points of the axes acknowledge the historical importance of dichotomies," but also whereby "the field itself is generated by the interplay *between* these end points" (196). Grosz's preference for the term *bodies* rather than *the body* inspires Hayles's turn to *embodiment*:

> In contrast to the body, embodiment is contextual, enmeshed within the specifics of place, time, physiology, and culture,

which together compose enactment. Embodiment never coincides exactly with "the body," however that normalized concept is understood. Whereas the body is an idealized form that gestures toward a Platonic reality, embodiment is the specific instantiation generated from the noise of difference. Relative to the body, embodiment is other and elsewhere, at once excessive and deficient in its infinite variations, particularities, and abnormalities. (196–97)

This idea of "specific instantiation" provides a crucial temporal element to Hayles's theory of embodiment. It links matter to time in order to conceptualize how materiality emerges in (or into) discourse. In effect, Hayles proposes something like an intersection of the *outside* and the *inside,* and she places embodiment at the elusive center of it. In doing so, she tries to theorize what resists being theorized: the interface between the two. Hayles suggests, then, that we sense embodiment, materiality, and other species of the *outside* in instances and intervals, at moments of disjunction ("generated from the noise of difference"). Once we have conceptualized them or even simply named them, they are *inside* and therefore subject to the vicissitudes of representation. But once inside, their imperfect fit ("excessive and deficient") implies their exterior origins.

The idea of a fleeting and ill-fitting relationship between the *outside* and the *inside* characterizes every act of writing. The difference between what Hayles describes and what I am trying to name lies in the question of intentionality. Hayles speaks to the idea of a relationship between words and things in themselves, and as a consequence her argument is an extremely important component of the perspectives on writing and agency that I want to develop. But to write is to apply, or perhaps to set in motion, particular manifestations of the relationship between words and things. An element of agency is present, and, as I noted above, it is precisely the focus—the reason for being—of composition studies, and the one most in need of theorizing at the moment. I think it is best theorized via *identity* if we can theorize it to take into account Hayles's and Hansen's concerns about *the outside* without its becoming an assumption or axiom—that is, something our theory takes for granted.

IDENTITY AFTER EPISTEMOLOGY

One way to do this is to let go of the idea that ontological stability is a prerequisite for agents. In the early 2000s, scholars interested in cultural identity tried to develop a workable theory in light of what Stuart Hall had summarized, in 1996, as "the anti-essentialist critique of ethnic, racial and national conceptions of identity" (1). These attempts at a new theory of identity, carried out under the name of postpositivist realism, took issue with various aspects of the postmodern critique of identity. They cited similarities between that critique and the modernist theory it had assailed. According to these theorists, identity is indispensable because it links the theoretical and the empirical, the conceptual and the historical. In other words, it links the *inside* and the *outside*. For these theorists, identity is a result of the fact that things happen to people and the fact that people try to make sense of these things. They argued that, when viewed strictly as a philosophical issue, identity can indeed be set aside, as it is in the postmodern critique, both because it carries too much baggage from its essentialist origins and because the particular moments of individuals' identity formations tend not to be of interest to postmodern theory, which is better equipped to perform systemic analysis on a larger scale. But by articulating and developing what I would prefer to call a neo-empirical (rather than postpositivist) theory, these writers hoped to reclaim identity not as a philosophical concept subject to various deconstructions but as a rhetorical act that helps offer insight into the persistence and ubiquity of identity-based cultural activity—including, I believe, acts of writing.

This attempt to retheorize identity begins with Satya Mohanty's "The Epistemic Status of Cultural Identity." In this article, Mohanty acknowledges "the accurate and damaging critique that postmodernists can make of identity politics," but he refuses to follow that critique to what he sees as its skeptical conclusion (32). Instead, Mohanty takes up a different notion of "experience" than that which he claims informs postmodern theory. For him, experience is not a function of ontology; rather, it "refers very simply to the variety of ways humans process information" (32). As a result, it "carries none of the normative baggage" associated with Hegelian notions of experience, nor does it differentiate between kinds of experiences (32). From this perspective, Mohanty claims, "we can construct a realist theory of social or cultural identity, in which experiences would not serve as foundations because of their self-evident authenticity but would provide some of the raw material with which we construct identities" (32). To consider experience "raw material" (or as data to analyze) is to consider it mutable or plastic, at once contingent and empirical. This makes it subject to political and historical action. For Mohanty, because experience is not an ontological given or an inevitability, it is not subject to the usual metaphysical difficulties and critiques.

Mohanty's empirical and deliberately nonmetaphysical theory of experience parallels, roughly, Victor Vitanza's distinction between traditional rhetorical theory and "post-philosophical Rhetoric" ("Critical" 42). In both, the idea is not simply to negate a philosophical critique but to recognize that the discussion itself—of identity in Mohanty's case, of rhetoric in Vitanza's—has taken place on the terrain of philosophy, and to offer alternatives. If the postmodern critique of identity is part of a larger, philosophically oriented mode of thought, then the neo-empirical perspective on identity does not reject that mode so much as show how it is beside the point. However, by retaining the very notion of experience and conducting his discussion in terms of epistemology, Mohanty's argument remains in philosophy's orbit. It accepts epistemology as such, treating it as something of a god-term rather than recognizing *epistemology* as just another feature of the discussion. Therefore, like Hansen's theory of technology, Mohanty's theory of identity can only take us so far toward a nonphilosophical theory of the *outside* because, at the end of the day, it accepts philosophical premises about the *outside* and uses a philosophical framework for thinking about agents and agency. Were we to apply this directly to the study of writing, we would be back on the kind of ground I think we should try to leave.

Starting from Mohanty's argument but venturing a bit farther afield from philosophical discourse, Linda Martín Alcoff's theory of identity argues that both modern and postmodern versions of identity are heavily invested in a Hegelian fear of the Other. Because of this fear, each sanctifies the individual as an epistemological unit on guard against the perceived threat of the social (333–34). In contrast, Alcoff believes that "this fear is itself situated, not existentially primordial," and that the "possible relationships that can exist between self and Other" under this rubric of fear do not "exhaust the genealogies of social categories of identity" (334). In other words, the Hegelian tradition that informs the postmodern critique commits its own form of essentialism: it mistakes social or political relations for epistemological ones.

For Alcoff, then, identity is irreducibly social and historical, which makes it political and rhetorical. In this sense, her argument shares something with Richard Rorty's critique of epistemology-as-philosophy in *Philosophy and the Mirror of Nature*. Despite their different political sensibilities, both Alcoff and Rorty see epistemology as a diversion of intellectual energy. From these perspectives, epistemology ignores contingency and its questions about time, context, situation, and relation. The difference, however, is that Rorty's answer is the recognizably philosophical gesture of asserting contingency's centrality in a general sense, while Alcoff pointedly places the social, political, and historical in the middle of the action, as it were, particularly in the process of forming not only specific identities but identity itself.

If we agree with Alcoff's political understanding of contingency, we open the door for rhetoric in the post-philosophical sense Vitanza describes. More important, we make way for a theory of how texts come to be, a way to think about agents as the boundaries of interiority and exteriority. We take a first step toward seeing *identity* as systemically or functionally necessary, perhaps even inevitable, in any attempt to account for what happens in an act of writing. If we treat *identity* as a result of social and historical relations and interactions (relations and interactions that include functional notions of interiority and exteriority) rather than as an epistemological concept, then we can also see that it is a (post-philosophical) rhetorical phenomenon.

Still, it might seem counterintuitive to propose *identity*, a term through which debates between modernisms and postmodernisms have been vigorously carried out, as a way out of the modern/postmodern philosophical framework that the study of writing has tended to inhabit. On the other hand, identity's rehabilitation might have been inevitable because, as Hall has noted, deconstructing a concept does not mean getting rid of it. According to Hall, concepts may be placed under erasure, "but since they have not been superseded dialectically, and there are no other, entirely different concepts with which to replace them, there is nothing to do but to continue to think with them—albeit now in their detotalized or deconstructed forms, and no longer operating within the paradigm in which they were originally generated" (1). This of course is my goal with *identity*. I want to retain and expand upon its connection to writerly agency while problematizing the traces of philosophical discourse that cling to it from various perspectives and critiques. In the next chapter, I will explore existing theories and applications of *identity* in greater detail. In this chapter, I have tried to set the terms for that discussion and the ones that follow by showing how our field's understanding of empiricism and its investment in exteriority (what I have referred to as the *outside*) are also at stake in the retheorizing of identity and interiority.

2

Everyday Iterability

THE EVENT-BASED THEORY OF IDENTITY I WANT TO develop should apply to any act of writing. In Chapters 4 and 5, I will "test" this idea by reading recent theories of invention and style through it, to see how it can influence our understanding of each canon. In this chapter, however, I want to show what light the theory can shed on the field's understanding of issues raised by contemporary writing technologies and practices. New forms and modes of textual inscription and circulation have beneficially denaturalized the act of writing itself, and in the process they have challenged disciplinary assumptions about what writing is and how it works. I want to show how an event-based theory of identity can participate in and contribute to our field's ongoing redefinition of writing, including its descriptions of what happens at the moment of inscription, at the beginning of writing.

Specifically, I think an event-based theory of identity can add to the field's ongoing effort to understand and describe the agency involved in an act of writing at a time when the question of technology has in turn raised questions about the subjectivity we take to be integral to any act of writing. Such a theory of identity challenges traditional notions of agency, even postmodern performative ones. In this chapter, I argue that such a challenge complements recent theoretical work on technology, and I show how, together, they offer new possibilities for talking, thinking, and studying writing apart from the requirements of either modernist sovereignty or postmodern performativity.

For almost two decades, theory and research in composition studies have shown how emerging, visibly technologized scenes of writing challenge the field's conceptual and pedagogical understandings of writerly subjectivity. This work has underscored the "remixed" quality of every act and product of writing. It has noted how technologies of writing make manifest the iterability that Jacques Derrida long ago identified as the fundamental feature of writing. In this condition of everyday iterability, words and other symbols combine and recombine unpredictably and uncontrollably, even in the hands of those doing the remixing. Conceptually, we in composition studies can see the individuals who produce such remixes as catalysts more than authors—relays that propel the unending process of signification toward an always receding horizon. And we are helped in this regard by a general perception of writing's increasing technicity; we can almost see writing's relentless proliferation and dissemination in front of us. Pedagogically, however, we still deal with the idea of relatively autonomous or consequentially intentional agents, even in the technologized scenes of writing that we have come to teach and be expert in. That is, even though we know that writing is complexly ecological, even though we know that signification is not a process with neat or even identifiable beginnings and endings, and even though we know that "it's signifiers all the way down," we also know that individual, empirical acts of writing begin and end. These moments might be mere punctuations, bumps in the otherwise smooth flow of difference, temporary and even illusory. But they seem to occur, just the same. And conceptualizing them is what an event-based theory of identity hopes to do.

It is important, then, for research and for teaching, to articulate a viable and functional figure of the writing subject amid the diffusion and dispersal of agency that characterize contemporary technologies of writing. As a field, composition studies cannot take the writing subject for granted; the writing subject cannot simply be a point of departure from which research and pedagogy proceed. Rather, the writing subject must be our very object of inquiry, the "thing" about which we are constantly trying to learn. And because, for our field, the writing subject is at once a theoretical construct, an empirical phenomenon, and a pedagogical object, it must be constantly reimagined and reinvestigated with this very multiplicity in mind. An event-based theory of identity bridges the gaps that exist among these different images of the writing subject, gathering them under one set of terms that speaks to the moment, at once conceptual and empirical, when writing begins.

COGNITION'S RETURN

The question of origins is not new to composition studies. We can see it in the field's interest in cognition during the 1970s and 1980s, which was an attempt to shed some light on the composing process by focusing on what feeds into it. Linda Flower and John Hayes were dissatisfied with "the mythology of discovery" ("Cognition" 22) that saw the moment of a text's emergence as shrouded in mystery and flattered with platitudes about creativity. Their use of thinking-aloud protocols was an attempt to "capture a detailed record of what is going on in the writer's mind during the act of composing itself" ("Cognitive" 368). They wanted access to "not only the development of the written product but many of the intellectual processes which produced it" (368–69). The idea was to trace, as closely as possible, the origins of writing in the passage from the preverbal to the verbal "within" the individual but without resorting to the romanticized language of discovery. As they saw it, at the moment of textual production the noumenal is rendered phenomenal through a mental act that is powerful and complex but not necessarily obscure. Like those whose romantic conceptions they wished to expand upon or replace, Flower and Hayes believed that writing "produces *new* insight and *new* ideas" ("Cognition" 22, emphasis added). Their model contained exteriority, interiority, and a vehicle for movement from the former to the latter, a vehicle they called cognition.

I think the criticisms of the model that Flower and Hayes generated were basically acts of resistance to a perspective on writing that seemed limited and limiting on the one hand yet descriptive and therefore useful on the other. The Flower and Hayes model was essentially informational. The idea that to write is to translate and transmit mental information is analogous to the idea, in information theory, that to communicate is to transmit a signal. Within such a framework, Flower and Hayes seem to have understood cognition not as a metaphor but rather as an empirical phenomenon. But composition's understanding of cognition has expanded and become much more sophisticated in the intervening years. In adopting a framework of distributed cognition—through activity theory or, in some cases, actor-network theory—empirical research in writing has asked a different set of questions about how writing acts take place. While it might continue to enshroud interiority as earlier cognitivist studies did, this research does recognize the idea of a porous boundary between interiority and exteriority. For example, in describing their approach to the writing of small children, George Kamberelis and Lenora de la Luna emphasize "three co-constitutive dimensions: *text*, the formal semiotic features of writing products, *context*, the forces (both proximal and distal) that exert effects on writing practices and products, and *politics*, the situated power relations involved in writing" (240). Presumably, these dimensions constitute one another in the context of the individual agent's decision-making process; thus the idea of cognition remains, but it is understood to be embedded within and influenced by a richer and more complex array of external forces and processes.

In *The Two Virtuals: New Media and Composition*, Alexander Reid tries to connect the implications of Deleuzean theory specifically to questions of cognition and consciousness, questions he considers central to composition studies, which, as he sees it, is "founded, implicitly if not explicitly, upon a theory of human thought" (97). Reid sees writing as "a fundamentally cognitive act, though significantly a cognitive act that is inextricably intertwined with technologies" (97). He examines two key features of composition's conceptual apparatus—cognition and consciousness—to see how they emerge from a recontextualization in systems of complexity and emerging technology. However, Reid's concern is less with cognition in itself than it is with cognition as a discursive function, an operation—one that we can continue to call *cognition*, for purposes of historical and conceptual convenience—that takes place in concert with other operations that make up the production, distribution, and reception of texts.

For Reid, Deleuzean theory and certain of its offshoots offer frameworks through which to articulate "a radically different theory of composition based upon a post-humanistic conception of cognition," a conception itself based on what Reid calls "the virtual-actual" (96). The "virtual-actual" describes "a process by which consciousness (and hence subjectivity) emerges from a continuous material space," by which one might develop "a mode of individuation and thought that replaces the traditional humanistic-Cartesian dualistic model, without becoming wholly captured within the logic of ideology or the will to technology" (96–97). A key feature of the virtual-actual is its rejection of "essence" as a useful conceptual category. As Reid explains, "the philosophical problem with essence is that it requires the existence of some external set of qualities or reference points on which materiality must be organized" (98). Except in the most faithfully (or dogmatically) Platonic schemes, these qualities do not exist; rather, they are categories developed by humans to organize experience and phenomena. But to describe reality with such categories is to digitize (i.e., render into discrete bits of data) a fundamentally analog world, thereby missing the continuity that characterizes it. In place of essence, Reid offers Deleuze's interpretation of Henri Bergson's *multiplicities,* a term Reid describes as "material processes in continual transformation." These multiplicities are composed, in part, of singularities, "attractors that draw in a range of potential fluctuations and bring them all to a single end point." Reid explains that "there are numerous types of singularities, describing different patterns of attractions, but fundamentally, they each function to create degrees of symmetry within a multiplicity" (101).

But of course cognition and consciousness (and, by implication, internalist terminology generally) must be retooled themselves. Toward this end, Reid's "virtual-actual" plays a crucial role, as it "deconstructs the internal-external boundary to map a continuous materiality" (23). If we recognize this boundary as being a historical and material artifact prompted by "the development of symbolic behavior," by symbolic behavior's externalization of memory, and by subsequent attempts to preserve the ontological integrity of the rational self in the face of this externalization (22–34), then we can see also that the boundary is itself a product of writing. Less abstractly, we can see that a continued emphasis on a rigid distinction between interior and exterior—extending even into twentieth-century cybernetics, which Reid describes as "a series of attempts to insulate human cognition from the implications of information theory" (57)—loses empirical relevance, as technologies continue to emerge and proliferate that make increasingly clear what has been the case since the very emergence of symbolic activity: that consciousness "is not so much the pinnacle of our internal self but the hinge, the point of interface, between internal processes and external networks of data, information processing, and technological activities," and that "in order to become conscious, one must articulate oneself through a network of distributed cognition" (30–31).

A RHETORIC OF THE INTERFACE

In *Lingua Fracta: Towards a Rhetoric of New Media*, Collin Gifford Brooke remediates classical rhetoric for contemporary technology, a gesture that turns away from questions of interiority and origins. Brooke also notes that "one of the defining missions of rhetoric and composition is its insistence on the social, cultural, and contextual position of the writer," an insistence that similarly works to "refute the traditional notion of the author/inventor" (62). This insistence is mirrored in the work of critics outside of composition studies who, despite "working from a different set of assumptions and writers," made similar claims about hypertext in the 1990s (63). These theorists described the writer as one who remediates, rather than creates, pieces of text. For example, in 1991, while surveying philosophy's attempt to account for intentionality in the "late age of print" and the emerging context of electronic writing, Jay David Bolter claimed that "there is no privileged author but simply textual networks that are always open to interpretation" (221). Likewise, in 1992, George Landow linked what he saw as hypertext's "transference of authorial power" to the poststructuralist idea (articulated, according to Landow, by such theorists as Roland Barthes, Derrida, and Michel Foucault) that "the self takes the form of a de-centered (or centerless) network of codes that, on another level, also serves as a node within another centerless network" (71, 73). In these early formulations, authorship was theorized as something of a relay through which the flow of information passes. The writer was figured as part of, rather than apart from, the textual/informational environment.

While early hypertext criticism made the *theoretical* claim that the new writing "was inherently incompatible with the traditional figure of the author," Brooke notes that composition studies confronts this figure "at the level of *practice*" (69, emphasis added). That is, in composition studies, the study of authorship is necessarily informed by the field's theoretical and historical origin in pedagogy, which remains at the core of its disciplinary identity. This commitment to pedagogy has necessitated a figure of the writer whose agency resides internally despite the acknowledgment, even the extensive mapping, of external constraints. So located, this agency underwrites the idea that writers can learn and be taught, that their writing can consequently develop and improve, and that they can ultimately gain greater awareness of and control over their writing processes. These pedagogical goals have defined composition studies since the beginning of the process/postprocess era, so much so that it is unproblematic to say that the student writer, more than the act of writing, has been the field's principal focus of inquiry.

According to Brooke, the problem is that neither composition studies nor hypertext criticism "ultimately manages to escape a print-based model of authorship" (63). Instead, both emphasize textual objects over medial interfaces, thus downplaying "the mutability of new media" and, by implication, missing the fundamental conceptual challenge this mutability poses to the study and practice of writing (6). In composition studies, this mistake is understandable because, as Brooke notes, "much of our theorizing about invention . . . remains bound by the particular media for which we invent, and for the most part we invent (and ask our students to invent) for the printed page" (68). But today, substantially and consequentially new material conditions of writing obtain: new scenes have emerged, new interfaces have proliferated. These postdate the initial theorizations of electronic authorship and composition's adoption of a sovereign writing subject, and they call for new terminologies with which to describe what it means to make a text. Composition studies can use its decades of experience dealing with student bodies to construct a figure of the writing subject with which new scenes of writing—new interfaces—might be theorized.

If new media technology allows (or requires) writing that eschews endings and beginnings, and if the distribution, circulation, and proliferation of texts overwhelms their erstwhile meanings, then according to Brooke a proairetic theory and practice of invention are urgently needed, and along with them a new figure of the writing subject. Brooke claims that "new media [encourage] us to consider a more radical distribution of individual attention, figured less as a decrease in authorial agency or power and more as a different activity entirely, one that exceeds authorship as we experience it in a print context" (80). This radical distribution requires a conceptual shift away from "the production and construction of meaning" as being central to the production and reception of writing (81). According to Brooke, "the various writing spaces that we might gather under the heading of new media offer frequent proof . . . both for a more social model of invention and for a model that is concerned more with practice than product" (82). Proairetic invention, then, with its "focus on the generation of possibilities, rather than their elimination until all but one are gone and closure is achieved," orients rhetoric away from the idea of individuals making "localized, conscious choices" (86, 116). This approach helps illustrate that questions of technological determinism (those to which the first hypertext theorists had succumbed) are themselves products of—and therefore relevant only to—analyses of the historical transition into print rather than the contemporary shift away from it. In other words, issues of agency, intentionality, and authorship matter most—matter only, perhaps—to and within studies of the medium that brought them to prominence in the first place. For us, as perhaps for the ancient Greeks (aside from Plato), questions of origins and essences carry less weight than do those of "function, value, and practice" (Brooke 196).

Less clear, however, is the need to retain the terminology of classical rhetoric, particularly that of its canons. While it is perhaps commonplace to complain that classical models are built on the idea of an individual, independent speaker; and while it has become increasingly clear that our familiar models of subjectivity—informed as they are by largely psychological notions of interiority—do not necessarily apply to Greek antiquity (as studies such as Susan Miller's *Trust in Texts* have argued); it is at least plausible to suggest that our current scenes might share some key features with those of "the Greeks." On the other hand, it is important to ask exactly what is gained by retaining a vocabulary that, while no more or less context-bound than any other, might carry a particularly problematic load of baggage, one that may raise more issues than it resolves. I will return to this question, and to Brooke's perspective on invention, in Chapter 4.

WRITING AS COMMUNICATION

In these attempts by Brooke and Reid to retheorize agency and subjectivity, a figure of the writing subject remains, as it should. Again, this is because of the field's roots in the matter of pedagogy, which has always directed the field's theoretical approach to writing. Unfortunately, a less salutary part of this legacy is composition theory's longstanding view of writing as primarily, even exclusively, a form of representation. It has understood writing to be a tool and a vehicle, one that requires a sovereign and intentional subject to "use" it. Because of this legacy, it will be very difficult to retheorize the writing subject without having retheorized writing apart from representation. I don't intend to pursue a nonrepresentational theory of writing; rather, I want to claim that the very ideas of representation and communication are overwhelmed by contemporary scenes of writing. They have always been overdetermined by the scenes of writing for which they were developed. But these ideas are of particularly limited use in describing the current scenes and interfaces, and therefore they cannot help the field arrive at a contemporary theory of the writing subject.

The proliferation of "communication" technologies makes this retheorizing at once more urgently necessary and more readily imaginable. Now, more than ever, the idea that writing is primarily a form of intention-laden communication, that communication is primarily the conscious reproduction of a predetermined content, and that *content* is itself a meaningful concept, is available for revision. We might begin this revision by recognizing that the very idea of information has a history and an ideology with which we should take issue. In this so-called information age, information's history and ideology threaten to become naturalized and reified, to the detriment not only of composition studies but of everyone who writes and otherwise "communicates."

The commonsense notion that writing is a technology by which ideas are represented and circulated pervades composition studies despite the fact that, in the 1980s and 1990s, various theorists in the field tried to bring "deconstructive" sensibilities to composition theory, research, and pedagogy. In 1985, G. Douglas Atkins and Michael L. Johnson's groundbreaking collection, *Reading and Writing Differently: Deconstruction and the Teaching of Composition and Literature,* offered variations on "a deconstructively based pedagogy that might at least help to do away with that insipid, padded, and inauthentic language that Ken Macrorie has epitomized in the term *Engfish,* which is nothing if not writing 'blocked' by the closure of simplistic and unexplored consistency, usually motivated by a desire to please a teacher who is perceived as expecting the same" (Introduction 4). In 1988, Reed Way Dasenbrock's "Becoming Aware of the Myth of Presence" used the critique of logocentrism (which he provocatively claimed to be "so pervasive that we must keep reminding ourselves that it is writing—not rhetoric, not invention, not inner speech—that we study and teach" [84]) to argue that then-current approaches to writing instruction conflated speech and writing, to the detriment of the latter. Also in that year, Jasper Neel's *Plato, Derrida, and Writing* carefully described—and acutely but constructively critiqued—Derrida's philosophical arguments against philosophical conceptions of writing. As Neel notes, the "key move" in Derrida's early work "is to 'deconstruct' the West's conception of 'communication' by showing how that concept begins with and depends upon the suppression of writing" (100). As a result, "writing theorists in the United States must understand his ideas and take them into account in some way, even if only to reject them" (100). Nearly thirty years later, it is still not clear that we have done so. Our theory of writing—our core set of assumptions about what writing does and how it works—remains communication-oriented, representational, and—given the current state of technology—marginal.

To some extent, there has been good reason for composition theory not to address writing beyond its communicative functions. For composition studies, the writing subject has an irreducibly material and pedagogical dimension that must inform any theoretical formulation. And while it is the field's object of study, it is also the field's conceptual point of departure, its founding figure. We meet writing subjects every day in classrooms and writing centers; for us, writing is a very specific and embodied activity, one that we encounter almost exclusively on pedagogical terrain.

WRITING AS INFORMATION

Ironically, the development of information technology has taken place precisely around a heightened notion of intentionality, one wherein information becomes an object to be manipulated rather than a temporal process. Historians and theorists of twentieth-century information technology have pointed out that the very tools we use to "communicate" and "inform"—indeed the very language in which we conceive and discuss those tools—are thoroughly informed by principles and assumptions derived from a historically specific model of communication universalized and now become almost transparent. These principles and assumptions, which Ronald E. Day summarizes as "the conduit model," emerge from a desire "to functionally define component parts of events and to operationally understand events in terms of representational systems that then can be used for management" (40, 39). An understanding of interaction (or mediation) as based on the rigid logic of code rather than the slippery movement of language contributes to a deep-seated vision of writing and communication as activities in which ambiguity and indeterminacy become problems to be solved rather than necessary and even generative features. According to N. Katherine Hayles, while theorists of language and writing note that "complexity was vested traditionally in the Logos, the originary point conceptualized as necessarily exceeding the world's complexity," in code, "complexity inheres neither in the origin nor in the operation of difference as such but in the labor of computation that again and again calculates differences to create complexity as an emergent property of computation" (41). Code, which at its core translates voltages into "unambiguous signals of one and zero," builds complexity and ambiguity by adding layers of programming (46). For Hayles, this is significantly and consequentially different from the idea—articulated in familiar critical terms such as *chora, différance, iterability,* and *the trace*—that complexity inheres in the system: "At the level of binary code, the system can tolerate little if any ambiguity" (46). Likewise, "in the worldview of code, it makes no sense to talk about signifiers without signifieds" because "every voltage change must have a precise meaning in order to affect the behavior of the machine; without signifieds, code would have no efficacy" (47).

As others have pointed out, this mathematization of information was intended to address a technical problem of telecommunication: how to accurately reproduce electronic signals. But in so doing, it gave rise to an entire ideology of information spreading far beyond the technical. That is, it cast all communication issues as technical issues. According to Tiziana Terranova, mathematician Claude Shannon and cyberneticists such as Norbert Wiener established the idea of *contact* as "the minimum condition for communication . . . a temporary suspension of the multitude of tiny and obscure perceptions out of which information emerges as a kind of fleeting clarity" (15). This contact, the ability of a signal to be produced, transmitted, and received at a separate destination without being altered, quickly came to be seen as the sum total of the communication problem. Terranova's characterization is worth quoting at some length:

It does not matter who the sender or receiver are, whether they are machines, animals, bacteria, genetic sequences, or human organisms. Reason and meaning, dialectics and persuasion, truth and falsehood are all temporarily evacuated from the scene. There is no longer an interlocutor or an audience to address, there is no rhetorical play of ideas, but a kind of bare set, where all communication is reduced to a drive to clear out a channel for transmission between two points separated by space and united only by the channel. From an informational perspective, communication is neither a rational argument nor an antagonistic experience based on the capacity of a speaker to convince a listener or to impose his perspective. (15)

By design, this system is closed. In order for it to work, factors that would interfere with or impede the reproduction of the signal are seen as structurally external and a threat to the success of communication. They are either for the signal or against it. And if they are against it, they are categorized as "noise." Recipients of signals become targets, not interlocutors, as the problem becomes one of getting the message intact through a hazardous landscape. Within this design, the idea of content becomes at once structurally irrelevant and substantively predetermined. Whatever the piece of "information" to be transmitted might be, its substance is formulated in advance, and in the process of communication, its integrity must be preserved in order to avoid chaos and breakdown. The question, particularly for composition theory, is the degree to which this technological problem—a problem of hardware—has influenced other areas: at what point and to what extent have issues of signal reproduction and noise interference—the latest iteration of the conduit metaphor—migrated to what Shannon would call the "semantic" dimension of communication?

I doubt that anyone in composition studies—teacher, researcher, or theorist—would assent to an exclusively or even predominantly operational view of writing. Certainly, we understand that there are writing technologies, and that people use them to interact with one another. We understand that an aspect of writing involves the reproduction of signals between discrete units across channels, broadly speaking. But at the same time, most of us work from the equally commonsense assumption that writing is a rich, complex, and human-oriented activity, one that cannot be adequately explained, studied, or taught as a strictly technical matter. Even our arguably most overdetermined genres, technical and professional writing, are understood to be not threatened but constituted by "outside" forces. This is, as Terranova suggests, the very heart of rhetoric. Yet despite our appropriately complicated understandings of writing, we implicitly subscribe to this ultimately limited perception of what it means to produce a text. The reasons are historical, cultural, political, and consequently understandable. But they no longer serve the study of writing and our understanding of the writing subject very well.

To some extent, the very fact that we have a model composed of internal and external dimensions, mediated by the body and/or the subject—and the fact that much of our theory, research, and teaching takes this complexity into account to some degree at least—guarantees that our understandings and descriptions of writing will never be given over completely to an informational, mathematized concept of writing. We will probably never reduce writing to the mere transmission of a clear signal (though some legislators, administrators, and so-called education reformers might). Nonetheless, we should not take this position for granted, especially in light of constantly emerging writing technologies that are designed from the very perspective that oversimplifies textual interaction. Ultimately, the problem with the conduit metaphor and the idea of information is a problem of language: that is, we forget—or never realize—that these are in fact metaphors, not direct perspectives on reality. In composition studies, we risk forgetting—or never realizing—that empirical description is a type of figurative language. Or we risk the equally bad mistake of assuming that since empirical description is inherently figurative it is not qualitatively different from any other kind of discourse about writing. In either case, we lose sight of the fact that metaphors guide our inquiry explicitly and implicitly, directing our attention toward certain questions rather than others in consequential ways. Thus, we might inquire about the degree to which *information* and *communication* "entitle" (in Burke's sense) the situations in which we use those terms. In turn, we might ask if other metaphors might direct us toward other, perhaps more pressing issues. Or, we might ask how best to proceed with these particular "entitlements," on the assumption that they can direct our attention in certain productive ways. But either way we will theorize with eyes open, as it were.

WRITING AS CIRCULATION

The everyday iterability of contemporary writing raises a key question about the relationship between production and circulation (or distribution). Is every act of writing merely the reassembling of available symbols and ideas, as evidenced by the strict and utter conventionality of words, sounds, and images? Or is there still, despite iterability's newly quotidian status, some irreducible quality in every single writing event, something manifested in but not tied to the conventional forms in which content or meaning are expressed? If the latter, then there remains a place for a figure of the writing subject, but theorized in light of the acknowledgment that an act of writing occurs in a particular moment of time, or that it constitutes a disjuncture of time, and that this moment/disjuncture is irreducible, inexplicable through recourse to iterability alone.

On the one hand, we can see what technologies such as handwriting, typing, word processing, and text messaging have in common, and we can see that the questions we might ask about them are the same composition studies has asked for years: What processes does the writer undergo? How are the resulting texts received? Are there generic features to which writers and readers adhere? How can we help people improve their writing in these forms? What counts as improvement in each of these forms? In this sense, *writing* seems timeless, quasimystical, always and only manifesting in but never essentially bound to a particular technology. This metaphysic—writing as such, we might call it—informs almost every discussion of writing, both in and outside of composition studies.

But now, the question is whether or not the current expansion and proliferation of writing technologies sustains, even solidifies, the idea that writing as such is a viable concept, one that continues to serve well as composition's object of study, or whether the expansion and proliferation of writing technologies finally exposes what had been the case all along: that there is no such thing as writing as such, that there are instead these contingent and unrecoverable moments or events of inscription. The specificity of each event requires a reconceptualization of the activity or idea that we commonsensically refer to as *writing*, now explicitly understood as the juncture of time and spacing, production and reproduction—not a hybrid of the two but a third item, a new theoretical apparatus: a theory of writing without writing.

Perhaps our students would not know what to make of such a proposition even though, ironically, their own practices illustrate its possibility. Yet it is precisely this relationship between what writers do—the various and ongoing ways in which they work with texts—and how we study what they do that needs to be clarified. In this sense, and as ever, the writing subject figured as the student writer in composition studies is no different from any other articulation: thoroughly textualized, i.e., immersed in deeply textual worlds, but not necessarily able to map those worlds coherently and with confidence in order to better participate in them. This is the longstanding premise and promise of composition studies, its reason for being. Only now it is writ larger than ever. Writing subjects are everywhere, not only or even most significantly in classrooms or other institutional-educational settings. Always and everywhere already connected, the writing subject is more integrated into circuits of inscription than at any time in the history of writing, and circuits of inscription are proliferating and becoming more complex. It should go without saying that people who study and teach writing must understand this situation as completely as possible. Likewise, it should by now be apparent that neither modernist nor postmodernist perspectives on writing and subjectivity provide the right equipment for the task.

However, from a theoretical perspective, the question is not how to avoid metaphors so as to describe things clearly and distinctly. Nor is it a question of merely acknowledging the irreducible metaphoricity of all symbolic interaction, especially (and ironically, if not perversely) when considering the symbols with which we study symbolic interaction. The first option is naïve, the second banal. From a theoretical perspective (which is also methodological), the question is how to avoid answering the question. In a sense, we cannot choose the literal over the metaphorical; we cannot even suppose that there is a substantial (that is, nonmetaphorical) difference between the literal and the metaphorical because, we quickly realize, *the literal* is a particular kind of metaphor: a metaphor of clarity, of unmediated communication, of noise elimination.

From a theoretical perspective—that is, from the point of view of trying to think about the problem of metaphor as it relates to the question of communication and with particular respect to writing—the best option, then, is to adopt a strategy of continual deferment or obstruction. We are not compelled to accept or refute the notion that the literal is possible, nor need we commit to the idea that it's metaphors all the way down. Of course, the very idea that we can either "choose" or feel "compelled" to arrive at some position on the question of metaphor in the study of writing is itself questionable. Our current equipment for thinking about the act of writing directs our attention to the twin poles of choice and compulsion. The goal should be to find alternatives.

So, on the one hand, there is a thing called "writing" that changes its trappings or manifestations over time and through new technologies; we imagine it to be different from technology, despite their intimate relationship. On the other hand, there are those moments or events of inscription, irreducible to and inseparable from technology. As I have suggested, composition theory can try to articulate writing in a third sense by articulating these two. But, actually, this is a false choice: a "moment of inscription" lurks within even the most iterability-oriented theory. In the end, iterability defers rather than dispenses with the question of the writer, and it was never meant to do otherwise. If anything, this deferral (specifically, this *différance*, which—we recall—neatly captures time and space in one utterance), this embedding of one theory of writing within another, suggests that what I have been calling the "act of writing" or the "moment of inscription" is inadequate. But is it necessary? Do we need it just the same?

I think so. *Writing* is our god-term, the center without which our ongoing discourses on writing—called, in turn, rhetoric and composition, composition studies, writing studies, or anything else we like—cannot proceed, without which they would be inconceivable. It is our field's ultimate scene, our "total context" (Burke, *Grammar* 143). It has no empirical dimension, if by empirical we mean without metaphor, without mediation. Because it is not empirical, neither does it "carry" or "transmit" "information." Consequently, notions of information and communication become not problematic but irrelevant; their dissemination as metaphors through the various professional and disciplinary discursive systems becomes a matter of historical interest, but it holds no consequences for the contemporary study of writing. This is because the study of writing is the study of the idea of a master trope—not of the trope itself, which, as a god-term, cannot be studied. Theorists in composition and rhetoric, in composition studies, in writing studies—all of us work not with a common metaphor, but with the idea of such a common metaphor. Despite having always worked in the field of writing, we have never actually studied writing and, in a sense, we never will.

But, as it turns out, the question is not exactly how to understand writing, or how to approach writing as an object of study. There is no choice in this. Because it is scenic (again, in the Burkean sense), writing is not optional, nor is its study. We cannot choose not to do it; that choice, assuming it could be made, would itself be an act on the scene of writing. Moreover, how we "understand" writing is equally irrelevant to the fact of writing. From a disciplinary perspective, this is perhaps troubling: if the purpose of rhetoric and composition (of composition studies, of writing studies) is to figure out ways to "understand" or "approach" or "study" writing, and if writing itself is not available for such activity, then what is there to do?

We might begin by trying to work out the theoretical implications of the prospect that writing is, as I noted, scenic, a god-term: unapproachable. From an empirical perspective, we can say that writing erupts (into) contexts, and we can examine how these contexts proliferate, become more complex. Perhaps the work at hand is to construct a discourse that recognizes the impossibility of accounting for writing while providing the imperative to do so anyway. In such a discourse, writing is the backdrop against which the activities of our field normally take place, one that we are always trying—and always failing—to apprehend. In such a discourse, the writing subject is always and only a contingent, elusive, event-bound category, and we will never catch up to it. But we still have to describe it.

3

Theories of Identity

I HAVE NOTED STUART HALL'S INFLUENTIAL PERSPECTIVE on the issue of identity after its "deconstruction" by postmodern theorists. He agreed with them in rejecting the idea of "an unmediated and transparent notion of the subject or identity as the centred author of social practice" (2). He argued that the postmodern critique had made it necessary "to rearticulate the relationship between subjects and discursive practices" (2). In fact, for Hall, it was precisely the dynamics of this relationship that made "the signifier 'identity'" indispensable (2). Furthermore, he pointed to the fact that identity was enjoying a "veritable discursive explosion" in the 1990s despite the postmodern critique. As he put it, while "the notion of an integral, originary and unified identity" had indeed been undermined, it was being replaced by the figure of "the endlessly performative self" (1). This was possibly a reference to Judith Butler's work at the time, which also accepted the postmodern critique and in turn offered the extremely influential claim that "identity is performatively constituted by the very 'expressions' that are said to be its results" (*Gender* 25). Throughout the 1990s, then, the question of agency in the era of postmodernism—particularly as it related to matters of race, class, and gender—was often answered by the claim that identity is performative, fluid. This assertion has endured in the first two decades of the twenty-first century.

In this chapter I trace the issue of identity as it has been taken up in composition studies. Specifically, I examine how notions of performative identity (and other nonessentialist theories of the term) have circulated in the field and the uses to which they have been put. Then, I extend this notion by theorizing identity in terms of the concept of the *event*. I have two goals in doing so. First, I want to call attention to the issues that complicate the use of *identity* as a concept or tool with which to study writing. Second, I want to use those very complications to retheorize identity for the study of writing. Writing has always been a complex activity, and studying it has always required what I. A. Richards called "speculative instruments" capable of handling such complexity. In contemporary scenes of writing, writing's complexity comes into sharp relief thanks to the technologies that produce and distribute it. I addressed these scenes in Chapter 2, and now I want to focus on making *identity* a better speculative instrument than it currently seems to be.

Like Hall, Butler, and many in composition theory, I accept the postmodern critique of *identity*. But I believe this critique prompts us to do more than adopt "performativity" as a modifier for (or of) identity. Instead, it calls for a theory that accounts more precisely for the relation between textuality (the *inside*) and exteriority (the *outside*). A performative theory of identity, such as Butler's, comes close to this accounting, but its approach to exteriority remains within the realm of the philosophical. By this I mean that it focuses on the fact rather than the function of the *outside*. In contrast, by theorizing identity as an event rather than a performance, I want to treat the idea of the *outside* as a crucial component of signification, one without which the very idea of signification makes no sense. In such a formulation, the nature or makeup of exteriority—the describing of which is the endgame for most philosophical discourses—is less relevant than its functionality. Such an approach trades ontology for rhetoric, and in doing so it complements composition's longstanding focus on writing's agents. As I noted in Chapter 1, the field has never thoroughly adopted postmodern notions of the *subject* because they seemed rooted in a fundamentally different set of concerns. These concerns were better suited to addressing writing at systemic rather than individual levels. That is, they could not accommodate the idea of materiality that composition studies needs in order to do its empirical and pedagogical work with writing's agents. But the concept of the *event*—or at least, a particular version of this concept—brings a conceptually viable form of materiality to *identity* while maintaining the emphasis on writing's systematic complexity that postmodern theories helped bring to the field.

IDENTITY IN COMPOSITION

For good reason, some in composition studies find *identity* to be a problem. For example, Diane Davis and Michelle Ballif offer acute analyses of identity along the lines of the postmodernist critique: Davis connects it to "the problem of idealism" and the idea of "the unified 'individual'" (30). Ballif locates identity on a foundation of violence—"the negation and appropriation of the other"—that forms the dialectical core of Western culture and history (4, 10). My aim, of course, is not to refute these arguments (in fact, I mostly agree with them) but to offer an approach to identity that avoids these problems.

Such critiques notwithstanding, *identity* finds a welcoming home in composition studies. Christian Weisser notes that from the 1960s to the turn of the century, identity played a key role in composition's major theoretical frameworks, despite profound differences among them. Each of these frameworks tried to develop "a more complex and sophisticated awareness" of how a writer's identity is formed. This awareness was then applied pedagogically, as writing teachers worked with students to "extend their identities" (85). According to Weisser, cognitivist approaches to writing saw "identity as emerging internally." Expressivist perspectives argued for "writing as an act that authenticates and affirms the self" (83). Eventually, constructionists "urged us to see identity not as something internal, singular, and centered, but as a language construct generated by discourse communities and used by them to maintain community coherence" (84). In the 1990s, the influence of "postmodernism, feminism, and cultural studies" prompted the notion that writerly identity is "the product of an array of social, political, and ideological forces" (85). Finally, Weisser himself argues that "identity emerges not only from our human relationships, but from the connections we have with other life-forms in an array of habitats" (87).

As a field, composition studies tends to use *identity* in two related but different ways. First, there is the concept of identity, or identity as such. We can see this in the Davis and Ballif examples above, and when Lynn Worsham refers to "the groundless ground of identity" (172). Second, there is identity as an empirical phenomenon or a lived experience, as when Anne-Marie Pedersen discusses "why and how people negotiate language and identity" (290). At times, composition scholars shift between the two uses of the term, as when Zan Meyer Gonçalves writes about "encouraging speakers to present their identities as multiple" while asking them to "foreground an agreement . . . around issues instead of around identity" (11–12). Similarly, Gail Shuck invokes identity-as-concept in a discussion of "the mutually constitutive relation between identity and agency," and she invokes identity-as-experience to note, in the next sentence, that "identities are multiple, dynamic, and shifting" (122). Scholars refer to identity-as-experience when describing markers that individuals or groups adopt, construct, or are burdened with. In contrast, identity-as-concept is usually the target of the postmodernist critique, though identity-as-experience (for example, in the notion of "identity politics") comes under fire as well. In fact, one problem with the critique of identity lies in the notion that the deconstruction of identity-as-concept necessarily invalidates any version of identity-as-experience. This is the gist of the countercritique offered by Satya Mohanty and Linda Martín Alcoff, which I highlighted in Chapter 1.

Because I am concerned with how our explicit theories and implicit assumptions about identity inform the study and teaching of writing, I focus on identity-as-concept. But precisely because the two uses of the term are related, I hope that my argument will influence how researchers and teachers deploy it to discuss "experience." In other words, while my argument is wholly theoretical, I don't want it to be of theoretical use only. In fact, as I argued in Chapter 1, the field could benefit from a more actively reciprocal relationship between theory and empirical research—a relationship that would, in turn, have implications for teaching.

At any rate, the very fact that identity continues to be contested tells us something about its evocative power for scholars, researchers, and teachers of writing. In this sense, *identity* endures as a term to think with, as Hall would say. As Weisser indicates, the field's understandings of identity have moved away from the essentialism implicit in cognitivist and expressivist frameworks. And even those frameworks had been somewhat "de-essentialized" by the middle to late 1990s, as works such as Linda Flower's *The Construction of Negotiated Meaning* and Thomas Newkirk's *The Performance of Self in Student Writing* explored, respectively, the social dimensions of cognition and the performative aspects of expression.

FLUID IDENTITY

Today, most compositionists would disavow an essentialist approach to identity. Generally, we prefer to see identity as enmeshed with, informed by, or resulting from a range of other factors that converge at the level of both the individual and the collective. Because of our interest in agency, we also prefer to see identity as something individuals can construct for themselves to some degree, through writing or other forms of symbolic action. And we think such a view requires writers to recognize the many cultural constraints under which identity construction always takes place.

For example, Marilyn Cooper offers a "nonessentialist" perspective on identity in which "the self is fluid and in process, determined by its experiences to a certain extent but still also constructed or chosen with varying degrees of awareness" (91). According to Cooper, in this version of identity the self is defined "not in opposition to others or to its community but in relation to others" (91). Cooper's discussion raises the specific question of cultural, racial, and ethnic identity, echoed in the work of other scholars before and since. Work along these lines acknowledges the idea of a nonessentialist theory of identity rather than dispensing with identity altogether. For example, Jaime Armin Mejía recognizes the poststructuralist critique, especially as it appears in the work of a composition theorist such as Lester Faigley. However, Mejía notes that in addition to language, "the 'social density' of one's life, or the lack of it, as created by kinships, works to construct one's identity" (197). Echoing this perspective that identity is connected to more than just language, Arnetha Ball and Ted Lardner note that "identity is ever in flux" (52). And they argue that while "the construct of identity negotiation allows teachers to take into account" the "social and personal locations" that students of color often occupy, it can also help teachers "examine how the ideology of race shapes our sense of self, including our professional identity as educators" (52). More recently, Ball and Pamela Ellis have also asserted identity's importance, citing work by Roz Ivanič and others and noting that "identity development is a dynamic and fluid process" that "can be fostered through practices like writing" (503). Similarly, Amy Burgess and Ivanič have reasserted a claim each had made previously: that "writing is an act of identity" (228). Like Ball and Ellis, Burgess and Ivanič see identity as something that "changes over time" (228). They then examine how "a single act of writing involves the coordination of multiple processes that exist on different timescales" (229). Likewise, Michelle Cox, Jay Jordan, Christina Ortmeier-Hooper, and Gwen Gray Schwartz collectively address the interaction of "language, identity positions, and material considerations," particularly with regard to second language writers (Introduction xx). Melanie Kill discusses "the relational nature of identity, which places individuals in the situation of depending on others to serve both as reference points and sources of validation for their presentations of self" (232). She uses this notion to draw a nuanced picture of the teacher-student relationship, which relies on an often problematic but nonetheless real desire for "relational stability" that teachers should recognize not only in their students but in themselves (232).

Likewise, Bronwyn T. Williams describes writing as "a deliberate construction and expression of identity" (Introduction 6). More important, he asks us "to reconsider how our intellectual theorizing about identity and the performance of self often falls short of capturing the daily human consequences of the identities through which we engage the world," and he urges us to "work with students to reflect on the identities we all bring to the academy from our lives outside and to understand where those identities connect or conflict with the literate identities recognized by the institution"

(8, 12). Perhaps Keith Gilyard puts the problem most succinctly and in its most appropriate political context when he points out that "it's useful at times to complicate notions of identity, but primary identities operate powerfully in the world and have to be productively engaged" (270). Moreover, he adds, "when we engage in discussions about fluidity, we ought to keep in mind the question of who can afford to be anchored to a focus on the indeterminate" (270).

These studies address the question of identity directly. They define, defend, or otherwise examine it as a concept, and they assert its relevance to the study of culture and society, writers and writing. But we find a more extensive and sustained theoretical engagement with identity in Donna LeCourt's *Identity Matters: Schooling the Student Body in Academic Discourse*. In this book, LeCourt tries to balance "the significant insights poststructuralism adds to our understanding of discourse and identity" with a "concern with how writing might function as a material intervention into the world" (7). Throughout, she recognizes and values the idea of a nonessentialist, fluid, and otherwise postmodern perspective on identity, and in this context she tries to create theoretical space for the materiality she considers unavoidable. "We don't live identity only in a discursive realm," she writes, "we live it in interactions with other people in cultural spaces continually overdetermined by material realities of poverty, racism, violence, and threat" (2).

To "mediate" between discursivity and materiality—that is, between the *inside* and the *outside*—LeCourt examines her students' literacy autobiographies, which offer evidence of a serious disjuncture between theory and practice. She notes that while, as a theorist, she understands "identity as fluid, as constantly changing and able to cross borders," through their writing her students articulate a very different perspective. These students' "sense of themselves as bodies . . . continually reasserts the cultural premise that undergirds so much of our society's identity politics: body = experience = thought" (21). They do not experience the fluidity of identity that postmodern theory calls for. Instead, their relationships with discursivity—with academic discourse, in particular—are marked by conflict and struggle. Their identity positions, whether chosen by them for forced upon them, are indeed mutable. But they are not arrived at (or resisted) through processes that either LeCourt or her students would call *fluid*. Looking at what her students write about their struggles with academic discourse, she finds that it has "a power that exists beyond the writers' control," a power "to inscribe the (student) writers as subjects of its power" (41). She believes, therefore, that composition studies needs a way to recognize this struggle, incorporate it into its theories and pedagogies, and ultimately help students contend with the power of discourse more effectively. In other words, the field needs a theory to account for "a world where rhetoric and the material are seemingly opposed" (22).

Toward that end, LeCourt turns to Hall's work on identity, particularly his use of the *suture* metaphor. Through Hall, she defines identity as "the meeting point of discourse and self wherein the subject makes a choice, influenced by other discourses and social relations, to invest in particular subject positions and take them on as part of identity construction" (38). For LeCourt, "the materiality of language itself" warrants such a formulation (39). Even though we might consider academic writing (the particular kind of symbolic action that her study emphasizes) to be primarily a discursive activity, it nonetheless "emerges from its material location in institutions of higher education" and cannot be separated from it (39). According to LeCourt, this materiality, comprising "textual practices and products," works upon the bodies of students, hailing them into new subject positions and identities (40).

More generally, then, identities and the desire for them are created though the body, which "becomes the relay point where discursive relations and material conditions meet" (86). For LeCourt, this runs counter to what she sees as the poststructural description of a purely discursive process of subjectification. Fortunately, she notes, composition studies is familiar with materiality thanks to its understanding of "how text circulates among bodies and through bodies" and its Burkean legacy of seeing rhetoric and language-use as forms of action (194). Our field sees writing as "the locus through which material and discursive relations act upon the subject" (194). Yet despite this familiarity, LeCourt claims that "we have paid much less attention to the *act* of writing itself as both discursive and material," and she urges the field to redefine writing precisely in this way (194–95). Because this act "engages the subject within the performative moment of language," it opens up a space in which that subject "can deliberately enact multiplicity within the space of enunciation" (198).

IDENTITY AS STRATEGY

The critique of identity emerges, in part, from a larger critique of dialectical thinking undertaken by various critical theories and philosophical ideas associated with postmodernism and poststructuralism. As I will discuss in Chapter 4, one aspect of this critique is that dialectic's emphasis on opposition and negation results in exclusion, which makes it a fundamentally violent process and a rather blunt instrument of analysis. For example, in his extended study of the philosopher Henri Bergson, Gilles Deleuze cites Bergson's critique of dialectical thinking, noting that "the concrete will never be attained by combining the inadequacy of one concept with the inadequacy of its opposite," and that "the singular will never be attained by correcting a generality with another generality" (*Bergsonism* 44). He prefers Bergson's concept of duration, which he defines as "a type of multiplicity that is not reducible to an overly broad combination in which the opposites . . . only coincide on condition that they are grasped at the extreme point of their generalization, empty of all 'measure' and of all real substance" (45–46). In a later work, Deleuze takes aim at identity in particular, claiming that, as a philosophical concept, it is something of a ruse that results from deeper, ongoing modulations between basic functions he refers to as "difference and repetition" (*Difference* xviv).

It is against this critical backdrop that rhetorical theorist Dana Anderson situates his study of identity. In *Identity's Strategy: Rhetorical Selves in Conversion,* Anderson points to "the virtual abandonment of 'identity' as a valid theoretical concept" (5). He notes that poststructural perspectives tend to see identity as "part of the problem, not the solution" to talking about individuals and agency.

But while he sympathizes, to an extent, with the critique of identity, he wants nonetheless to retheorize it in order to preserve the valuable insights he believes it can still offer to the study of rhetoric, even in postmodernity. In turn, a rhetorical perspective on identity is potentially relevant to composition studies, and not merely because rhetorical theory is one of our field's neighboring (often overlapping) areas of inquiry. Because Anderson believes that identity should "hold a place within rhetoric's critical vocabulary of the person," his examination of identity's strategic dynamics offers a way to think about the actions of individual agents, another abiding concern of composition studies (6).

Anderson theorizes identity as fundamentally situated, dynamic, contingent, and temporal. In doing so, he ventures somewhat further than previous notions of identity as performance. Specifically, he sees identity as a question of action, of doing more than being. Following Kenneth Burke, he calls attention to the irreducibly dialectical operation that sits at the core of any human activity, and that is made possible by the fact of language. He does not quite argue that identity is an emergent property or feature of language. Rather, his argument suggests that *identity* names a site of emergence, a place where exteriority (the *outside*) appears in or through language (the *inside*). Eventually, I will take this line of thinking a step further and argue that language creates the very conditions for conceiving of exteriority and its emergence into language in the first place. But for the moment, Anderson's argument is worth tracing at some length, especially those aspects of it that make use of Burke's writing on identity and identification.

Anderson's argument that "identity matters less as something that one 'is' and more as something that one *does* in language" seems to echo Butler's theories about identity-as-performance (4). And, in fact, Anderson acknowledges that his claim is not necessarily new. But insofar as he wants to highlight "identity's rhetorical functions" in order to make it a "deliberate, more precisely explored area of rhetorical theory," we might say that he wants to articulate identity with rhetorical theory in order to transform the latter (5). In this spirit, he chooses to treat identity as a discursive or narrative phenomenon more than as an ontological state, or, as he puts it, "as a word not for what a person or self 'really' is but rather for a person's ability to articulate a sense of self or self-understanding" (6). Moreover, according to Anderson, "rhetoric needs identity not for what it might say or occlude about what we 'really' are but rather for what it might reveal about how language moves us" (13).

For Anderson, "the driving force of all symbolic action" is what Burke referred to as the "'ritualistic naming and changing of identity'" (15). Anderson sees Burke as "the theorist who has most influenced . . . rhetoric's more general thinking about identity" (15). Burke referred to identity as a problem, but Anderson argues that he did so quite differently than do the postmodern theorists with whom he is otherwise thought to share a great deal. Borrowing a term from philosophy (perhaps by way of cultural studies), Anderson suggests that it might be better to think of Burke as engaging with a *problematic*—that is, as "a dynamic, an economy, a perpetual interplay between the individual and the world by which both shape, and reshape, their senses of who they are" (32). Approaching identity in this way requires "our continued interest in probing human symbol use to find the spots where this 'problem' arises, where grammatical, rhetorical, and symbolic transformations of identity can and do transpire" (33). As Anderson sees it, "concocting some means to establish—or abolish—identity" runs against the grain of Burke's attitude, which emphasizes transformation, ambiguity, and dialectic as fundamental features of human activity in symbols (32).

For Burke, dialectic is the mechanism by which identity necessarily takes place. Timothy Crusius notes that Burke's approach to dialectic focuses particularly on the importance of terms and terminologies. Therefore, "to attack dialectic is to attack the self-conscious study of language" (31). Dialectic—the inexorable process of merger and division, which for Burke is built into language use—gives identity a dynamism and contingency that essentialist notions of the term cannot account for. In other words, for Burke, identity makes sense only in light of its inevitable and continual disintegration and reintegration; as a term, it derives its power precisely from this dynamic. According to Anderson, Burke sees the problems identity poses as evidence of "its social indispensability, its generative role in language and human relations" (32). In contrast, he notes, "poststructuralism proposes to 'solve' the problem of identity . . . by doing away with it completely" (43).

At a glance, there seems to be a contradiction between Anderson's emphasis on the experiential dimension of identity and his adherence to Burke's focus on language over reality. The appeal to experience is, in many ways, an appeal to the idea of something that is precisely not identical or reducible to language but that may be rendered in language. From a postmodern or poststructural perspective, the relationship between experience and language is the very issue at hand, and this issue serves as the main basis of the critique of identity. Therefore, to the extent that Anderson acknowledges the idea of experience, he endorses the notion of an ontologically private and nonlinguistic (or nonsymbolic) realm that feeds but is not the same as—and that certainly does not originate in—language. And yet, in following Burke, he also indicates an acute awareness of the complexity of any possible relationship between symbolic action and the motives such action would represent. Anderson and the "postpositivist" theorists I discussed in Chapter 1 share a similar goal, which is to bring a viable and sturdy concept of exteriority to bear upon theoretical discourses that would otherwise have little or nothing to do with it. In the context of the study of writing, this is my goal as well, which is why I propose an emphasis on the event. Such a focus offers a way to shake identity loose from its essentialist heritage while retaining its conceptual and explanatory power.

It may be that I am reading too much into Anderson's text. After all, his concern with conversion narratives indicates transformation more than emergence, a change of status rather than the creation of status as such. Yet, insofar as *conversion* for Anderson "refers to a change in the circumference of an identity . . . signaled by a corresponding alteration of the god-term or 'ultimate motivation' that this constituted identity seeks to realize," it necessarily involves novelty, the presence of something that had been absent (130). Moreover, this emergence is not the result of willful action or rational deliberation. Writing about Deirdre McCloskey's description of her epiphany of gender certainty, Anderson notes that "it is not a conclusion that he [then Donald McCloskey] induces from the collective details of his gender-ambiguous past and then decides to act upon; rather, it is a new understanding about himself that he realizes and to which he then submits" (130). The novelty that prompts change or conversion comes from elsewhere; it is a new element erupting into a situation that then transforms the situation. It is an event.

THE EVENT

According to the philosopher Alain Badiou, *event* is one of the names for "a pure Outside" (*Logics* 381). However, as Quentin Meillassoux (a student of Badiou's) notes, the idea of "an outside which was not relative to us . . . existing in itself regardless of whether we are thinking of it or not," has become rather difficult to think, imagine, or discuss with the equipment of contemporary philosophy (7). Consequently, philosophical work on the *event*—such as that of Badiou, Meillassoux, and in a different way, Deleuze—tries to put as fine a point as possible on the nature of the *outside*. For me—and, I believe, for scholars and teachers in composition studies—such inquiries might provoke agnosticism at best. This is because regardless of any particular philosophical perspective, the important issue is that the *outside* will be evoked, regardless of how we define or understand its nature. That is, it will be represented textually (i.e., on the *inside*), even if only in statements asserting that it cannot be represented. From the perspective of the study of writing, and from a rhetorical perspective more generally, this is its most salient feature. For composition studies, it is enough to know that a quality of exteriority (of some kind) is named by the term *event*. Knowing this, we might then be prompted to try to understand how this quality functions in discourse and to see how, defined somewhat more specifically as *event*, it might illuminate individual acts of writing, particularly when we consider it in relation with our handy and hardy term for examining writerly agency: *identity*.

Once again, Derrida's perspective from the margins of Western philosophy opens a door for composition studies. In "A Certain Impossible Possibility of Saying the Event," published after his death, he raises a set of familiar concerns about the inevitably written or enunciated quality of any event, and therefore of the very idea of event. He traces the complex relationship between *outside* and *inside,* particularly the difficulty raised by the impossibility of contemplating the *outside* without resorting to textuality—that is, without bringing it *inside.* The analysis leads him to view agency as less performative than symptomatic, a distinction with consequences for composition studies as we try to comprehend agency in light of writing's increasingly empirical complexity.

Derrida begins by stating some fairly standard views of the *event:* that it must, by definition, be "unforeseeable" and "absolutely singular" (446). He notes also that speaking of the event is not the same as experiencing the event itself. As Derrida puts it, "the saying of the event . . . lacks . . . the event's singularity simply because it comes after and it loses the singularity in generality" (446). Derrida then characterizes the event's necessary singularity as also its condition of impossibility: anything that can be foreseen—that is, anything that can be imagined or understood, anything that can be articulated in terms of already existing conditions—cannot be impossible: "A predicted event is not an event" (451). We can speak of an event after it has happened, but in order for it to have been an event, we cannot have known or guessed or supposed that it was going to occur. For Derrida, one consequence of this impossibility is that we "cannot say the event in theoretical terms" (452). That is, we cannot do with the event what theory does with its various other objects: make statements about them that apply across the board, particularly toward future occurrences. This would seem to present a serious problem insofar as we would be "utterly disarmed . . . baffled in face of the always unique, exceptional, and unpredictable arrival of the other, of the event as other" (452). However, he notes that such a situation is "never pure or absolute," and at this point some familiar Derridean themes begin to emerge (452).

Derrida argues that the event's supposed singularity is actually haunted by repetition. Just as "a word is comprehensible only because it can be repeated," so "the event cannot appear to be an event . . . unless it is already repeatable in its very uniqueness" (452). In other words, an event comes to sense *as* an event *in terms of* or *in light of.* This is to say that it is relatable, that it is in relation. Because of this, the event "can only be greeted as a return," like that of a ghost (452). More prosaically, we can say that this quality of uniqueness is functional or symptomatic rather than empirical or ontological. But regardless of how we characterize that uniqueness, what begins to emerge is the idea that, because of this original iterability, the event always has the quality of an utterance. That is, the familiar distinction between the event and the speaking about it (the distinction with which Derrida had begun his discussion) is deconstructed—not eliminated or dismantled but problematized to the point where the idea of a boundary between the *outside* (where the event comes from) and the *inside* (where it can be identified and spoken or written of) cannot be taken for granted. And, in turn, this inability to take the boundary for granted will have to be the basis for any future theory of the event. That is, the very idea of such a problematic boundary will, in and of itself, function as the ongoing and animating difficulty at the heart of every theory of the event.

After laying out this problematic, Derrida considers the issue of will and agency. For him, the condition of impossibility that characterizes the event necessarily "exceeds [his] ability and power" and "transform[s] the logic of decision" (454, 455). The event and "the will to power" are at odds because wanting is itself an act of control, and so it is subject to the movement of repetition and iterability: "If I want what I can want, [then] what I can want . . . is commensurate with my decision" (454). On the one hand, a decision is "a sort of expression of my power," but if it can only be carried out within the range of the possible, the recognizable, the iterable, then it "does not interrupt anything, it does not tear at the fabric of the possible" (455). According to Derrida, a decision that is also an event must be one that is not undertaken but undergone. Agency in this sense is functional or symptomatic, a part of the apparatus of saying the event, though not necessarily the determining part. The symptom is "a signification of the event over which nobody has control . . . that no conscious subject can appropriate or control, either in the form of a theoretical or judicative statement, nor in the form of a performative production" (457).

Ultimately, if the event is always already a saying—that is, if an original iterability constitutes the event and does not merely represent it within discursivity or textuality—then the event is functional or symptomatic, too. That is, the event happens *within* or *in terms of* the qualities of uniqueness or singularity. In this sense, *event* and *agency* take part in the same general system of iterability or discursivity, though they have different functions. *Event* contributes the function of an exteriority that propels general discursivity, maintaining the sense that things (the *outside*) and words or other symbols (the *inside*) are separate but attachable to each other. *Agency* contributes the function or symptom of consciousness, of decision making—the idea that there can be control over these attachments.

IDENTITY EVENT

If we think of identity as something that happens detached from human intention yet within the realm of human action, and if we see it as a necessary feature—perhaps *the* necessary feature—of discourse, then we might begin to conceptualize acts of writing as moments in which a writer's agency is neither sovereign nor constricted but, rather, functional or symptomatic. In other words, my interest in identity for the study of writing has less to do with who writers think they are at moments of inscription than with the various dynamics at play during those moments of inscription. To be sure, it is useful and even necessary to say that those dynamics involve, in some measure, whatever agency we might attribute to a given writer during a given moment. But I do not want to equate functional or symptomatic agency to the conscious or sovereign agency that is much more familiar to composition studies. If we do this, we will risk overlooking useful ways of thinking about writing subjects—writers—that can contribute to richer understandings of the increasingly complex scenes in which writing takes place.

With this in mind, we might start to think of identity not as conceptual equipment for studying writing nor as a conceptual obstacle to the study of writing. Rather, we should think of identity as a feature, a function, a symptom of every act of inscription, at work in every scene of writing. From such a perspective, the questions about identity's modernist heritage and its postmodern deconstruction remain as intractable as they have been, but in a way they are also beside the point. They remain intractable insofar as modernism and postmodernism continue to set the terms for discussion of such key concepts. They are beside the point insofar as we recognize modernism and postmodernism as discourses of a certain era or epoch, discourses whose ability to make sense of contemporary scenes of writing seems to diminish with every new complication of those scenes, discourses that imagine representation—rather than, say, relation—to be the primary purpose of writing.

Still, we can relate this idea of identity as a feature, function, or symptom of discourse to our established notions about identity's social and personal dimension in writing. As I noted in the introduction, we now usefully integrate our field's tradition of attending to the social dimensions of writing with its tradition of studying the cognitive processes of writers. We do not think of these as necessarily separate and distinct areas of inquiry, and as a result, we can easily think of identity as a sociocognitive phenomenon that is expressed or performed in writing. If we now go further and start to think of identity as I have been articulating it here—that is, as event—we will begin to acknowledge, more fully than our field usually does, the extent to which writing *constitutes* more than it merely *reflects* or *represents* the terms, conditions, and contexts in which communicative interactions and relations happen among actants (to borrow a term from Latour in *Reassembling the Social*) of all sorts—human and otherwise. This does not mean that we stop studying and explaining how identity is expressed or performed in writing. But it does mean that we can start studying and explaining how identity also exists *in* writing. For that matter, we might even explore possible relationships between these two views of identity. But in any event, one important prospect that emerges from this new perspective is the idea that identity, as such, is itself a necessary object of inquiry: a concept to think *with*, to be sure, but also—and perhaps more important—a concept to think *about*, when we are thinking about writing.

4

Distributing Invention

IF IDENTITY IS AN EVENT, AND IF THIS EVENT occurs *in* writing—that is, if identity is a feature or symptom of writing itself—then we should treat identity as something more than a concept with which to think. More than something to think with, identity is something to think *about,* something to take into account, when we study and teach writing. Thinking about identity, we would see it as part of the ongoing problematic that the study of writing tries to address, and that the teaching of writing tries to explain. In fact, we might say that if we are not thinking about identity when we think about writing, then we are not dealing with writing in its fullest complexity. At the same time, I do not think the question of identity in writing can ever be resolved. Rather, I think we should understand it to be an ongoing theoretical, empirical, and pedagogical concern—something that helpfully complicates our theories, studies, and pedagogies of writing. For example, it can help us theorize the spaces of interiority left relatively untouched even by our most sophisticated approaches to writing. As I have noted in previous chapters, without an account of the relation between interiority and exteriority, composition studies cannot really capture writing's complexity.

More than any other canon except perhaps style (which I discuss in the next chapter), and particularly in its modern understandings and uses, invention deals with origins and interiority. This is the case even when invention is theorized, as we will see below, socially and relationally. In what follows I examine some recent, theoretically sophisticated theories of invention. I show the spaces they illuminate on the way to offering more complex views of writing, and

I note the spaces they pass over. I do not intend these examinations as critiques. Rather, I want to underscore the limitations inherent in our vocabularies for talking, and therefore thinking, about writing. And I want to offer a way around these limitations, through the theoretical discourse of identity I have been developing.

THEORIES OF INVENTION

Contemporary theories of invention address the complicated question of agency in contemporary writing. In different ways, these theories have tried to account for the fact that writers live and work in complex environments. They have tried to account for the fact that those environments provide more than mere backdrops or scenes in which intentional acts of writing take place. Implicitly and explicitly, these theories indicate that the categories of the pentad laid out in Kenneth Burke's *Grammar of Motives* tend to blur—even more than Burke himself allowed for—when we contemplate how acts of writing actually happen. According to these theories, contemporary communication technologies highlight features of writing and rhetoric that, until now, have been obscured by print's technological dominance. This is why they venture further conceptually than does Burke's description of the ratios and relationships among the pentad's terms. In so doing, they prompt new theoretical questions about the nature and functions of agency. They raise questions about other terms and concepts that composition studies brings to bear on the profoundly reimagined rhetorical situations they describe. And they offer new metaphors for thinking about contemporary scenes of writing.

These new metaphors for the contexts and conditions of writing challenge us to develop equally new ways for describing how an act of writing comes to be, particularly through the mediation of an individual writer. For while ecological metaphors for writing and rhetoric enrich our sense of the contexts in which an act of writing comes to be, they tend to leave the agents implicit in such metaphors relatively untouched. I have been contending that identity enriches, by complicating, our thinking about such agents.

The theories I review here all propose models in which a subject who writes is one component among many others. This imagined writer is not at all a sovereign agent acting upon a passive scene. Yet this subject also reflects our field's theoretical and historical investment in an agent who is not entirely enmeshed, at least not in the last instance. Because of this, these theories preserve a version of what Robert P. Yagelski calls a "Cartesian view of writing" (*Writing* 43). But, again, my purpose is not to criticize these theories. In fact, it may be that our field's investment in the image of an empirically available writer who is also a sovereign agent requires any new theory to preserve this image in some form, however implicitly. In a sense, this image is our disciplinary lifeblood. It informs our field's unique perspective on agency, prompting us to ask questions that other areas of humanistic inquiry have asked but have only been able to answer abstractly. Because of this, the idea that some notion of Cartesian sovereignty might remain, even in such thoroughly ecological metaphors for writing, is not necessarily a theoretical problem that needs to be solved. Rather, the problem we should focus on is what to make of that sovereignty—or rather, of the *image* of that sovereignty—in contemporary contexts: contexts that make propositions of sovereign agency rather difficult because they stress the profound interconnectedness of every component; contexts that grant equal status to each element on the scene of writing. The persistence of an image or idea of sovereignty troubles our current ecological metaphors for the complexity of writing, in a good way. It keeps us honest, so to speak, by reminding us that while our students are indeed enmeshed, they are also individuals. The question is, and has been, how to reckon theoretically with this paradox.

INVENTION AND NOVELTY

Invention has been of special interest to composition studies at least since the field decided to treat writing as a generative activity, one that produces rather than merely transcribes thoughts, emotions, and ideas. But by claiming that writing produces something—and that, therefore, invention is important—we also raise questions about novelty itself. And we ask the theoretical and empirical question that animates this book: where does writing come from? Addressing this question requires us to consider carefully the relationship between exteriority (*the outside*) and representation (*the inside*) that I discussed in previous chapters. Invention, then, provides a context for exploring the problem that my theory of identity seeks to address: how to discuss writing's agents in ways that acknowledge, simultaneously, the theoretical challenges raised by poststructuralist theories of the *subject* and the empirical exigencies of composition's scholarly and pedagogical emphasis on the *writer*. I am not necessarily trying to rethink the interaction between agents and the scene of writing, since contemporary theories of invention already do this. Rather, I am trying to theorize, or describe, the idea of the writing subject. I am trying to open the black box of agency, as it were, by applying language to what might be going on "in there," during the writing act. Questions about the relationship between interiority and exteriority animate this book, finding in the topic of agency their most acute expressions. But ironically, and according to the terms of identity as I have theorized it, in order to get into the writing subject we have to get outside of agency. And in order to do that, we have to question not only theories of invention but, ultimately, the very idea of invention.

While scholars in composition studies have theorized invention in different ways, Janice Lauer notes that the term generally refers to "the initiation of discourse." Longstanding questions exist about "whether invention is individual or social" and about "whether writers exercise agency in inventional activity or whether they are written by these acts" (*Invention* 3). But even though, according to Lauer, "major rhetoricians and their subsequent interpreters have disagreed over the nature, purpose, and epistemology of invention," and even though these disagreements can be profound and consequential, it seems that when theorists, researchers, and teachers in composition studies invoke the term, we mean the means by which some kind of novelty appears, and this meaning holds for contemporary scenes of writing, which are often characterized as sites where novelty is understood as the repurposing or remixing of old symbols (*Invention* 11).

As I noted in the introduction, by *novelty* I mean the idea that something comes to be which had not been: a nontrivial quality of newness, whether in the eye of the writer alone or according to the views of a broader set of readers. Such a notion of novelty seems implicit whether we believe that acts of invention occur individually or collectively, or whether we think of them as being distributed across time and space. That is, we hold a similar assumption whether we believe that invention names the process by which intentional individuals mine their knowledge and experience for unarticulated ideas, or whether we believe that invention is a group effort through which collective wisdom is funneled through semi-intentional individual acts of writing, or whether we believe that invention is a systemic operation upon which it is well beyond the capacity of any individual to exert an intention. In each of these cases, we subscribe to the notion that *something* comes to a text, appears in a text, or moves through a text—something that is not of that text, that has existed or continues to exist outside the text. Even if we think of invention as remixing (that is, as the rearranging of previous texts) we still implicitly proceed as if *something* guides, or at least influences, the remixing process. Whether we locate that influence within or beyond the writer (perhaps in the chaos of contexts that make up any given scene of writing, including contexts created by writing or language itself), we think of it as different and in this sense apart from its textual manifestation. As I argued in Chapter 1, language itself seems to bear this dynamic, forcing all of us to be empiricists of a sort who function as if words represent or manifest things straightforwardly, even when our theories prompt us to question that very idea.

Because our field is committed to writing's agents, we have tended to place the source of that influence in the individual. Even our most social and collaborative theories have supposed or imagined an intentional agent. I do not intend to argue against such an imagined figure. Instead, I want to offer a way to describe and discuss that figure that comports with what contemporary theories of writing and rhetoric have to say about the symmetrical complexity of writing's contemporary scenes.

GENRES OF INVENTION

Anis Bawarshi's *Genre and the Invention of the Writer* is an ambitious attempt to answer a question very similar to the one I propose in this book. Specifically, Bawarshi wants to know "what happens *to* writers when they begin to write" (1). He approaches this question through invention and genre, arguing that a sophisticated theory of the latter can lead to an expanded notion of the former. A broader theory of invention, according to Bawarshi, would help address the field's mistaken tendency to see the writer as a conceptual "point of departure" rather than the meeting place of various discourses and desires (13). By defining invention as "the site at which writers obtain, negotiate, and enact specific social commitments, orientations, and relations," he hopes to derive implications for the study and teaching of writing (13). Among these implications is the idea that writing takes place within "a larger sphere of agency" in which the writing agent plays a part, though not necessarily the determining role (51).

Bawarshi correctly notes that most process theories and practices of writing see the writer as "the primary agent of invention" despite the crucial role such theories have played in identifying invention as a generative activity (60). In other words, process theory acknowledged writing's cognitive dimensions while downplaying or perhaps ignoring its social or generic complexities. According to Bawarshi, "process-based views of invention . . . continue to imagine the inventing writer as a cognitive free agent," one whose internal mental activity is subject to scholarly scrutiny and pedagogical intervention but whose location in social and discursive webs is relatively unexamined (68). As a consequence, invention is understood to take place between the ears, as it were, or perhaps in a general realm of discourse that lacks enough empirical and theoretical specificity to be of use. In contrast, Bawarshi argues that invention "begins when a writer locates himself or herself within the discursive and ideological formation of a genre and its system of genres" (72). As he sees it, invention's fullest complexity is best grasped when we understand that the boundary between the writer's internal operations and external situations is porous and heavily trafficked. Genre thus serves as Bawarshi's metaphor for describing where, as it were, this traffic takes place. The writer stands at the center or intersection, serving as both "an agent of his or her own actions as well as an agent on behalf of already existing social actions" (76). When we take this scene as the locus of invention, according to Bawarshi, we are "extending the sphere of agency" beyond the will or intention of the writer, and we are getting closer to describing what actually happens when texts come to be (76).

By theorizing invention as a relation between a writer's cognition and the environment, Bawarshi extends the implications of the social view of writing that has dominated composition studies for over two decades. Specifically, he extends Karen Burke LeFevre's argument for the sociality of invention by offering a terminology with which to articulate such a sociality. Urging the field to consider invention via "the habitat in which the writer functions," Bawarshi posits a dynamic relationship between habitat and writer, an ecology that can be analyzed and theorized (via the terminology of genre) rather than merely assumed. In so doing, he refines our theoretical apparatus not only for the study and teaching of invention but for the study and teaching of writing more generally. Bawarshi's theory lets us say that acts of writing emerge from identifiable locations in which individual writers participate, and from which individual writers' sensibilities are formed. Such a formula makes for a more detailed metaphorical description of how writing takes place than we might otherwise have.

Yet there is a sense in which the writer's sovereignty endures. A writer who can "locate himself or herself within" any kind of formation (be it discursive, ideological, or generic) is a writer who preexists that formation and who therefore functions, to some extent, apart from it. In this sense, even though we say that invention occurs in the complex interaction between writer and environment, we still reserve a conceptual space in which the writer, in the last instance, stands alone. As a result, even a theory of invention as distributed and ecological as Bawarshi's maintains a consequential distinction between writer and environment, between agent and scene, even as it analyzes that relationship closely. To maintain this distinction between writer and environment is to favor or privilege the writer. Yet I do not see this as a flaw in Bawarshi's argument. It makes more sense to say that the problem lies with the terms of discussion: with novelty itself and, by implication, with invention. And it is a problem composition studies cannot address solely with postmodern or critical theory.

As I noted in Chapter 1, our field faces particular theoretical challenges and opportunities that stem from its historical commitment to pedagogy. This commitment orients us toward materiality (or toward an image or idea of materiality) in ways that other areas of English studies do not necessarily experience. We make assumptions and analyses about embodiment that are informed by our uniquely student-focused mission. As a result, our theoretical, empirical, and pedagogical discourses unfold differently, even when they are informed by sophisticated theoretical formulations. For example, Bawarshi insists that writers can and do contest "representations of who we are and how we should behave," but then he adds that we do so not by claiming "some inherent identity" but by "engaging other genres, which draw on other subject positions and desires" (110). This leads him to the familiar claim that "identity is always plural and always in the process of presencing" (110). I believe our field's orientation toward materiality all but forces Bawarshi to say this. He must attend to the body of the student writer. More to the point, he must attend to an idea of absolute exteriority upon which our deeply held notions of writing and pedagogy are based, and upon which composition studies is based. He must—as we all must—respect the idea of the empirical even while adopting a postmodern theoretical discourse that calls the idea of empiricism into question.

Conundrums such as this emerge when we work from the assumption that identity and agency (and now, genre) are extralinguistic phenomena or have extralinguistic dimensions. Like the performativity metaphor, the genre metaphor clears a discursive space in which it becomes possible to talk about an agent who stands within yet apart from a scene, who performs an intentional albeit constrained act of writing. But in such a scenario, drawn in this way, writing is still denied its formidable and constitutive power. It reverts to being a medium, a mechanism of representation, a vehicle with which to convey *something* from the supposed outside of language. Like any other metaphor we might use to theorize writing, genre loses its explanatory power the moment we forget it is a metaphor. As Bawarshi would probably agree, genre does not explain or describe writing directly. Genre offers a vocabulary, a nomenclature (to borrow once more from Burke) for talking about writing in a certain way—one of many. My point is not that we should therefore abandon genre but rather that we should see it as a good deal more unruly and unpredictable than expressions of genre theory might let on, precisely because of its metaphorical nature. Having done that, we might then examine how the dynamics of interiority and exteriority that we thought characterized genre are actually the dynamics that characterize writing itself.

INTERFACES

According to Collin Brooke, composition studies tends to approach the five canons of rhetoric as categories when, actually, it should understand them as relations. In such a context, invention can be said to treat "the relationship between given and new information" (44). Relationality leads to the idea of "an ecological model of invention" in which one agent's "conscious, visible activity" is not necessarily the focus of analysis or pedagogy (44). Instead, Brooke emphasizes attending to "the conditions under which invention takes place" (44). In such conditions, various factors contribute to the production of what will be called "new information." Placing undue theoretical or empirical emphasis on only some of those factors—specifically, the mental and rhetorical activities of the human ones—reinforces the idea that the difference between writers and their environments is relatively firm. For Brooke, the ecology metaphor "encompasses more than the individual or social development of ideas" (45). It offers a way to think of how the production of new information is a more profoundly collaborative activity than we might have imagined.

Brooke cites previous studies of invention that have moved the canon beyond a focus on the individual. Among these are LeFevre's

Invention as a Social Act, which retheorizes invention away from "the tendency to think of it as either something that necessarily 'begins' with the individual writer or that ceases with the final revision of a particular product" (64), and Bawarshi's study, which emphasizes the extent to which our internalization of genres blinds us to the fact that "our agency is distributed well beyond our own particular articulation of it" (66). The question of distribution is particularly important. According to Brooke, our field tends to ignore the materiality of distribution even when it recognizes the mediated nature of social and symbolic activity. In other words, even when we accept that invention occurs in relation rather than in isolation, we have not carefully considered how those relations take place. We focus instead on the results.

Referring to Roland Barthes's distinction between hermeneutic and proairetic codes, Brooke sees our focus on results as essentially hermeneutic insofar as it "relies on the relative sturdiness of a final object and the negotiation of meanings within it" (68). Hermeneutics "operates through the establishment of an enigma, void, or mystery—an absence—that will be fulfilled eventually, but is held in suspense." It emphasizes meanings within or behind a text. In contrast, proairetics "indicate[s] actions or events" (75). It addresses the mechanics or "empirics" (Barthes's term) that lead to a text's production (75). Brooke argues for an approach to invention that would be built on the idea of an equal and dynamic relation between hermeneutics and proairetics.

Such an approach is particularly well suited to new-media environments, which prompt us "to consider a more radical distribution of individual attention, figured less as a decrease in authorial agency or power and more as a different activity entirely, one that exceeds authorship as we experience it in a print context." New-media environments encourage us to see a text as "the actualization of possible connections" (80). Brooke notes the existence of "many new media 'texts' that do not 'mean' in the same way that we might argue that a particular poem or essay means something." These texts do not necessarily represent a new development in the relationship between language and meaning. Rather, they highlight features of the relationship between language and meaning that print technology's emphasis on stability and textual artifacts prompted us to deemphasize, particularly as we developed our theories of invention. These theories, "which focus almost exclusively on the production and construction of meaning," need updating. According to Brooke, such updates will require increased attention to "the technological, as a site of distribution within an ecology of invention" (81). They will also require more concern with practice than with product (82). In addition, Brooke's discussions of Greg Ulmer's heuretics and Eric Charles White's kaironomia, as well as what he refers to as Jean-François Lyotard's "commitment to the *je ne sais quoi*," emphasize the aleatory potential of invention, the idea that an act of writing is not principally the solving of a problem or the transmitting of a message (though these things might happen) but rather the exploring of possibilities.

And although he does not cite Donald Murray, Brooke's approach to invention echoes that scholar's work as well, in ways that are relevant to the question of identity. Murray writes of "a constant revolt against intent" that is the core of the writing process, when that process is properly understood as doing "much more" than "recording or communicating" (6). Like Brooke (and like all of us), Murray knows the inadequacy of a theory that sees the writing process as a list of steps to be taken from the beginning of a thought to its completion, a list of steps that can be traced backwards for pedagogical purposes. As Murray famously notes, "process can not be inferred from product any more than a pig can be inferred from a sausage" (6–7). Like Brooke, and like others, Murray is concerned about the fact that in order to study writing, "we must stop time (and therefore the process) and examine single elements of the writing process in unnatural *isolation*" (7, emphasis added). The process of writing is "a process of interaction, not a series of logical steps" (7). We might even say that the following passage describes an example of proairetic invention at work:

> The volume of material we gather—consciously and subconsciously—becomes so immense and is so diverse it demands *connecting*. We are compelled to provide some order for the confusion of information or it will drown us. We must dis-

criminate, select the information that is significant, build chains of information which lead to meaning, relate immediate information to previous information, project information into the future, discover from the patterns of information what new information must be sought. The connections we make force us to see information we did not see before. The connections we are making also force us to seek new, supporting information; but of course, some of that information doesn't support—it contradicts. So we have to make new connections with new information which in turn demands new connections. These powerful, countervailing forces work for and against each other to manufacture new meanings as we live through new experiences. (12)

Murray's description of how writing happens does not emphasize technology. But in the first sentence, he articulates an orientation toward mechanical reproducibility (and the abundance of information afforded by it) that resembles Brooke's basic stance toward information and communication technologies, a stance Brooke explicitly derives from Ulmer and contemporary new-media theorists. In the rest of the passage, Murray describes a process that emphasizes connections made on the spot, as one goes along. It is an uncharted, potentially chaotic movement through textuality.

I compare Brooke and Murray to point out that our field has understood writing to be relational for decades, even when it was celebrating the writer's expressive singularity. And likewise, our more recent descriptions of writing as distributed, enmeshed, and ecological retain some sense of isolation or separation, the black box to which Janis Haswell and Richard Haswell refer. Of course, within Murray's detailed description of writing's relationality, we expect to find a singular writer asserting agency, deciding to do one thing and not another. But as it happens, even in the most thoroughly distributed process of invention that Brooke's approach could accommodate, we would find as well a figure endowed with some measure of decision-making power.

As with my discussion of Bawarshi and the genre metaphor, my purpose is not to expose a flaw in Brooke's theory. Rather, I want to highlight what seems to be a persistent feature of writing: agency. In doing so, of course, I am not calling for an attempt to directly observe this agency. But I do want to develop a plausible theoretical account of it, using the conceptual equipment I am trying to articulate. In that account, we would describe agency by depicting the interdependent relationship between interiority and exteriority, something that a distributed or relational theory of invention might not be built to do on its own.

VITAL EMPIRICS

Where Bawarshi looks to expand invention through genre theory and Brooke seeks to make invention a more relational concept than it has been, Byron Hawk brings vitalism and complexity theory to the table in order to highlight invention's beneficially unruly potential. In *A Counter-History of Composition*, he attempts, first, to "disconnect vitalism from its placement with romanticism and expressivism" in order to "examine its relevance to contemporary pedagogies of invention" (4). Building upon this, he then argues for "a new paradigm built around complexity" in order to arrive at "a post-dialectical understanding of contemporary pedagogies of invention for the emerging scene produced by digital technology" (7). Hawk recognizes that technological changes in the ways people write have scrambled the scene of writing for those who study it. These changes have allowed questions to emerge about writing and rhetoric that the field had not been forced to consider too carefully.

Specifically, Hawk believes that a more open-ended notion of invention is theoretically and pedagogically necessary in contemporary scenes of writing. Hawk's interpretation of vitalist traditions invokes some of that openness and argues that, in the past, it had been suppressed in the field's dominant theories. He takes particular issue with what he sees as Richard Young's and James Berlin's reduction of invention "to pre-established heuristics" that result in preordained outcomes (10). These heuristics work within fairly narrow conceptions of cognition and context that might have been appropriate for scenes of writing in which a multitude of ambient influences, pressures, and convergences could be factored out, given the fact that the tools of literacy had been relatively stable for decades, even centuries. But contemporary technologies make manifest the inherent fluidity of the rhetorical situation, and so they underscore the increasingly ill fit between themselves and our traditional theories of invention. These traditional theories—and, perhaps more important, the assumptions that inform them—no longer provide a suitably complex lens through which to think about, study, or teach contemporary writing in contemporary contexts.

Hawk turns to Paul Kameen and Ulmer for theoretical and pedagogical orientations that "situate student bodies in complex ecological environments" and use these situations as "an epistemological basis for invention" (10). Hawk notes that for Kameen in particular, "the body is the critical, epistemological link between situation and invention" (120). Inventional activity does not take place strictly between the ears—that is, within the consciousness of the individual. As with Bawarshi and Brooke, Hawk's unit of analysis from which to develop theories and pedagogies of invention is not the writer alone but the writer in complex context. This approach is more appropriate to "a contemporary vitalist paradigm of complexity," one in which the writer is one component among many, and where interactions and relations among various components are facilitated more than ever before by technologies of writing and other forms of symbolic action (10). It offers a better way to arrive at and account for "the ambient, unconscious, habitual elements of invention" that contemporary scenes and technologies of writing lay bare (169).

These new elements (or, more appropriately, these newly foregrounded elements) call attention to the fundamental connectivity that characterizes any interaction. They make it possible, even necessary, to think of interaction less as an exchange between discrete agents and more as a "movement through networks" of people, things, and ideas that are constantly assembling, disassembling, and reassembling differently (194). The result is a more comprehensive picture than any description of a specific scene of writing can capture. In fact, it is a transformation of the very idea of a scene of writing. As Burke suggested through his notion of pentadic ratios, all relevant components are in play and must be accounted for. But where Burke's view of relations envisions humans as the principle agents (despite their being variably constrained and empowered by the pentad's other elements), today's scenes of writing require us to be more expansive. In other words, at the level of network or system, it makes less and less sense to assert that decisions originate in individual people. In fact, it makes less and less sense to assert that decisions originate at all, since constant transformation and recirculation are the empirical norm.

If this is the case, then rhetoric's ability to describe discourse would seem to diminish. Rhetoric becomes instead another component or feature of discursive action. According to Hawk, rhetoric is less a framework or a theory superimposed from without than a participant in the ongoing processes of transformation. We might say that rhetoric is more functional than epistemological. As Hawk sees it, "if the entire ambient constellation of equipment establishes a continuously emerging world, rhetoric cannot be read as theory application, which is simply an instrumental operation. A theoretical idea or a particular technique is only one element within a larger constellation that produces an idea or action" (194).

Because invention is a component of rhetoric, according to Hawk we then have to reconceive it as "the mapping of these networks" (195). Specifically, invention "must start with the structure of particular constellations and the invention of techniques for and out of those specific occasions" (206). Hawk argues that composition theory "should be striving to develop methods for situating *bodies* within ecological contexts in ways that reveal the potential for invention, especially the invention of new techniques, that in turn reveal new models for action within those specific rhetorical ecologies" (206, emphasis added). One key is to rethink the role and value of heuristics, adapting them to the paradigm of emergence and transformation that contemporary writing and technology underscore. For Hawk, this means seeing heuristics as "parts of larger constellations rather than as abstracted general procedures" (208). Heuristics in this sense are not "generic, mental strategies that function unproblematically in any given classroom situation"

(249). Rather, "they are enacted in particular contexts and through particular methods that reveal or conceal elements of a situation and enable or limit the way students interact with and live in that distributed environment" (249).

Hawk's reference to bodies raises a question about the limits of dissolving the subject/object framework that informs invention, rhetoric, and writing. In the complex and emergent ecology of writing that Hawk tries to describe, bodies take up space, along with many other elements or components. All of the elements interact in ways that make it impossible to attribute agency or intention to any single source, even a human one. Human bodies in this sense are not preeminent; they neither possess nor wield an ability or characteristic that distinguishes them from the rest of the ecology. As with Brooke, what matters are the relations, the interactions and combinations that take place and in so doing produce novelty. But in this scenario, invention seems necessarily a feature of what Victor Vitanza calls the "future-anterior" (*Negation* 43). Invention describes the processes whereby novelty *will have been produced*. That is, we will be able to look back, as it were, and say that a certain relation, a certain combination, brought forth novelty. In other words, if we understand bodies as strictly empirical features of exteriority, as ecological items with no particular interiority of the kind we normally associate with subjects (or agents) and writers, then we cannot propose to predict the direction of flow. We can only look back to where the flow came from. As Hawk notes in his critiques of Young and Berlin, an approach to invention that predetermines outcomes, or ranges of outcomes, is itself a product of dialectical thinking, reflecting an unreconstructed understanding of the subject/object.

But Hawk's bodies are not only ecological. They retain a measure of interiority, due in part to Hawk's investment in vitalism. As a result, they preserve invention's prospective or predictive function, its tendency to look forward to relations and combinations not yet realized. They also bring Hawk's theory back, partially but crucially, into dialectical thinking and the subject/object relation that his theory tries to reconfigure.

For example, Hawk uses Ulmer's notion of "the conductor" to refigure writing's agents relationally. Hawk explains that "as conductors we are active initiators of movement and organization, passive conduits that allow discourses and forces to pass through and reconnect to other circuits and function in new machines, and participants in constellations that are co-responsible for our conduct" (255). This attempt to preserve the capacity to initiate and participate, despite being mediated by the capacity also to receive, indicates a reserve of agency that is not necessarily exposed to the ecological economy. But we have no precise way to think about or discuss how it works, and therefore no way to gauge the extent of its relatedness and interactivity. It is one thing to say, with Hawk, that "we are our accidents and our connections as much as our choices" (255). But it is another thing to say something precise about how these accidents, connections, and choices combine to form the various instances of "we" that Hawk's discourse is required to adopt. In other words, without an idea of how "we are" these various features, we slip back into the dialectical subject/object relation that distinguishes between agents and scenes.

Hawk pushes the subject/object question almost to its breaking point, thanks mainly to the theoretical resources he synthesizes and adapts. He rehabilitates vitalism and interweaves it with complexity theory in an effort to rescue invention from the back-and-forth of dialectical thinking. As I mentioned in Chapter 3, dialectical thinking is a common object of critique in various strands of poststructuralist theory, and Hawk draws on these resources as well, particularly on Gilles Deleuze. The result is a model of continuous and unpredictable relation and interaction among components, relation and interaction that in turn generate new occasions for continuous and unpredictable relation and interaction. Compared to the relatively rigid and agonistic movement of dialectical thinking (or of its caricature, at least), in which subjects make claims and counterclaims, Hawk's model for communicative interaction and invention more closely resembles Deleuze's "lines of flight," whereby, according to Hawk, "desire and vital impulse" set conditions for the emergence of "creative novelty" and the disruption of order.

According to Hawk, lines of flight represent "breaks in the material flow" of dialectics, of Aristotelian entelechy, of any mode of orderly development, progression, or invention, in order to generate "new combinations, new machines, new forces, new desires" (282). These breaks need not be initiated by subjects alone: in fact, they cannot be. The idea that subjects alone can act, individually or in concert, is perhaps the main illusion that print technology helped to foster as it isolated, fixed, and internalized—within the human subject's "mind" and on the relatively static page—the functions of reading and writing, separating them from each other and from the complex ecologies in which they participate. To the extent that contemporary writing, communication, and information technologies reunite these processes and recombine these components, they call attention to the problematic nature of the subject/object model undergirding our established theories of writing, rhetoric, and invention. They create the conceptual and pedagogical exigency that Hawk's theory addresses.

As I believe it should, Hawk's theory keeps faith with our field's commitment to a certain view of writing subjects and materiality. But in doing so, it also inherits the theoretical problems and opportunities this commitment presents. Hawk puts a fine point on these problems insofar as he exposes the extent to which this commitment is itself premised on a fairly rigid subject/object model, but his own language—particularly his treatment of *bodies*—indicates that the model will not go quietly.

AMBIENT INVENTION

In *Ambient Rhetoric,* Thomas Rickert explains that "invention is customarily understood to be something a human subject does, causes, or wills" (95). Like Bawarshi, Brooke, and Hawk, he aims to construct a model of invention that deemphasizes individual, subjective agents and focuses on holistic, distributed processes. To do so, he turns to the notion of *chora,* whose origins in Western thought lie in Plato's dialogue *Timaeus. Chora* (or, alternatively, *khora*) has been taken up in recent decades by poststructuralist theorists trying to address the concept of origins within a general context of iterability (which I described in Chapter 2). The ways these theorists engage *chora* shed light on Rickert's own attempt to recast invention. And according to Rickert, they prompt us to reconsider invention's function as a canon of rhetoric. Where traditional theories of rhetoric treat invention as either an analytic or a heuristic—that is, as a concept or category to be applied to situations—a choric approach to invention problematizes invention itself. From this perspective, what we call *invention* is not a framework for considering the elements in a given rhetorical situation. Instead, it is yet another participating element in a rhetorical ecology. This claim echoes Hawk's proposal to place rhetoric itself within rather than outside of the scene of writing.

But we have not yet transformed invention. This is because, according to Rickert, "much rhetorical theory still relies on a separatist mind/body/environment paradigm" (43). Consequently, the models of invention emerging from this theory emphasize order, a specific notion of space, and a particular form of subjectivity: "One must have a plan, or more interactively, an encultured aptitude, for capitalizing on the proper moments; a method for achieving a plan or a battery of practiced stratagems; and a spatial arrangement or layout reflecting the plan or strategies." From this point, "one then works as a rhetorical agent via ideas to achieve effects in the world 'out there'" (43). But theoretically and practically, such a model does not reflect the proposition that "minds are at once *embodied,* and hence grounded in emotion and sensation, and *dispersed* into the environment itself, and hence no longer autonomous actants but composites of intellect, body, information, and scaffoldings of material artifacts" (43). Especially in the hands of poststructurally oriented theorists such as Julia Kristeva, Jacques Derrida, and Ulmer, *chora* "transforms our senses of beginning, creation, and invention by placing those activities concretely within material environments, informational spaces, and affective (or bodily) registers" (45). Because of this, a model of invention based on *chora* is potentially more comprehensive than a standard model rooted in *topoi*. It recognizes the distributed agency and creativity that have always characterized symbolic action, nonsymbolic motion, and the various forms of interaction and interanimation between the two.

Rickert's first example of this interaction, and of his notion of ambience, is the caves at Lascaux and the drawings they contain. These caves "have general ambiences that help constitute work placed there, the spatial properties at particular spots yielding the sounds desired, a long round reverberation here or a short, clipped echo there. Without those properties, the human design for the caves would not be possible" (6). On the one hand, we might say that human actors (subjects) acted upon the cave walls (objects), using them as media with which to evoke or represent things, ideas, or emotions as images; they brought aspects of exteriority into representation on a surface (and in an environment) that served primarily as a tool or vehicle. On the other hand, we might say that all of the elements in this situation played a role in the articulations that took place, we might defer judgment on which if any of the elements were active (subjects) and which were passive (objects), and we might even balk at drawing firm lines or boundaries between the elements. One reason for taking this latter option is that, in theory at least, it promises a more fine-grained description of how new articulations—that is, novelty—might occur. It also offers to beneficially dislodge us from the anthropocentric perspective that our analytic traditions and our very use of symbols tend to foster. These last two concerns find expression in—and to this extent Rickert finds common cause with—certain scholars in science studies (such as Bruno Latour) and in posthumanism, respectively.

Chora gives conceptual texture to these notions of interaction and ambience. It signals not the origins of ideas but the paradoxical idea of origin itself. In this way, it functions more as a principle or problematic than a concept. In analyzing Derrida's discussions of *chora,* Rickert finds a "struggle . . . against understanding production and invention exclusively within the horizon of representation" (62). If representation describes the process of bringing exteriority into textuality or symbolic action, then we might say that representation offers a restricted and noninteractive model of how novelty comes to be, one more attuned to *topoi* and their concern with the material and metaphorical places from which novelty arises and with the agents (subjects) who find or "invent" it. In contrast, *chora* is concerned not with where novelty comes from or what novelty is but rather with the ineffable yet intractable dynamics of the very idea of novelty.

In poststructuralist terms, *chora* is aporetic. It names a thing, but the thing it names is that which creates the conditions for naming. In this sense, it is the origin of naming, the beginning of language, discourse, and writing. *Chora* names the idea that there is a "moment" when exteriority is invoked, textually or symbolically. But unlike *topos, chora* is not oriented toward human agency, at least not exclusively. Rather, *chora* seems to name a quality of inventiveness that is a feature of symbolic action itself, a property of symbols. And symbols are all we have to deal with, even when we want to discuss the very idea and the very content of an extrasymbolic realm. *Chora* is the name for the thought that there might be an ultimate source of signification, even as we understand that the notion of an ultimate source of signification is itself a signifier; it is not an index of something "out there," either in the material world or in some other imagined space.

When he turns to Ulmer, Rickert sees "a more complete flowering of the *chora* as a rhetorical concept," achieved through "a high degree of self-reflexivity" that is "appropriate for the electronic age, where near-total mediation, feedback loops, co-adaptive systems, and ecological systems theory are culturally and epistemologically ascendant, if not dominant" (67). Ulmer practices choric invention in order to generate "rhetorical production from our circumambient environs," which can be characterized by "the radical expansion and externalization of memory in cultural discourses, electronic networks, and databases" (68, 69). These environs, and the practices of invention appropriate to negotiating them, together create and require an understanding of place as "dispersed and distributed" (268). This new sense of place connects to "a sense of dispersion for the human subject that extends the insights of French poststructuralist thought" (69). For Rickert, the "emplacement of invention within the ambient environs displaces the priority traditionally assigned to subjective human activity for invention" (70).

Given an ecology characterized by dispersion and distribution, in which the boundaries between scene and agent are fluid, and in which transformation and emergence are ongoing processes, a theory of invention that works from stasis and differentiation will fail at the task of describing writing. Much more appropriate, Rickert argues, will be a theory and practice of invention that is attuned to flux, even to such a degree that it regularly calls invention itself back into question. But even this ecology necessarily reserves space for interiority, for a trace of agency or sovereignty that is not just a result of unexpected or radically adaptive recombinations of scenic components. We can see this trace in Ulmer's work.

Ulmer has always carried out his extensive theoretical engagements with poststructuralism in the service of pedagogy. At least since 1985, he has been concerned with "the inevitable transformation of the discourse of schooling in the age of mechanical reproduction" ("Textshop" 38). So it is not surprising that a sovereign agent lurks in his exemplary grammatological retheorizations of invention. In Ulmer's work the act of writing is reconfigured not only by poststructural theory but by technological change, and the result is a profound shift in what it means to make a text, or even to think about making a text. But there is always an agent, and that agent always makes decisions. He or she makes them in ways that are attuned and appropriate to the expectations, epistemologies, and vicissitudes of the contemporary cultural and technological moment—or, at least, that is what education is supposed to teach him or her how to do. But the agent remains, and for good reasons that coincide with those of composition studies. Ulmer's pedagogical imperative is to have subjects participate in the institutions of which they are a part, in which they are enmeshed. His goal is not to "deconstruct" writing subjects but to enhance students' capacities to interact.

In this sense, even though the idea of distributing invention across ecological components and across space and time is appropriate and necessary given the prevailing technological conditions (in parts of the world, at least), such an idea nonetheless does not— and in a sense cannot—speak to the exigencies that move an individual writing subject to make certain decisions rather than others, decisions that result in one text rather than another. In other words, while we can draw increasingly intricate theoretical and even empirical maps of the various streams that flow "into" individual writers, and while we can do the same kind of mapping for the symbols and texts that flow "out" of them, what happens within remains uncharted. And so we still lack the vocabularies, the nomenclatures, to describe every aspect of writing as thoroughly as possible.

CONCLUSION: INSIDE OUT

As I mentioned at the beginning of this chapter, invention raises the question of interiority, even when it is theorized socially and relationally. The theories of invention I have reviewed describe writing in new and beneficially complex ways, but they leave the idea of interiority relatively untouched. In doing so, they illustrate not their own limits but those of our current vocabularies for talking and thinking about writing. If even our most sophisticated theories of invention preserve traditional notions of interiority and exteriority, then perhaps we need to acknowledge the extent to which our discourses are influenced by the terms we inherit. Few of us imagine ever finding neutral terms with which to theorize and study writing. But neither do we fully consider the implications of that fact. At some level, we understand that terms and symbols (verbal, visual, and otherwise) are all we have. We know that they are our only equipment, ultimately, for studying terms and symbols. But it is not clear that we know how to theorize in light of this fact, particularly at this moment, when writerly agency is as opaque and mysterious as it has ever been despite our sophisticated theories.

If, as Burke notes, "all members of our species conceive of reality somewhat roundabout, through various *media* of symbolism" (*Language* 52), then this "reality" must include interiority and the agency that lies at least partly therein. In a sense, then, it seems uncontroversial to suggest that interiority is a feature of symbol making, a function of writing. It is a term, one that refers back, as it were, to something apart from writing that writing itself mediates. We might say that to see interiority this way is to approach it rhetorically. It is to stop looking beyond the term itself for that which ostensibly animates it and to suppose, instead, that the term itself animates its own "beyond," or at least the idea of it.

This view of interiority mirrors the approach to exteriority (or the *outside*) I described in this book's introduction. If adopting a functional rather than an absolute or philosophical exteriority allows us to think about writing more systemically than we otherwise might, then taking on a similar attitude toward interiority might help us retain the term's use while discarding some of its problems. In order to develop a more thorough theoretical vocabulary—one that would allow us to think and talk about writing's origins in greater detail—we might map onto interiority (and perhaps invention) the theory of identity that I have articulated. As I explained in the previous chapter, we can theorize identity as functional and symptomatic rather than essential or even performative. And with the complexity it thus acquires, we can articulate the idea of a dynamic between interiority and exteriority that constitutes not only acts of writing, but writing as such.

5

Conclusion: Theory as Method

IN THE PREVIOUS CHAPTER, I FOCUSED ON invention because of that canon's emphasis on origins. I wanted to show how even the most thoroughly relational theories of invention make space for an unaccounted-for interiority—Janis Haswell and Richard Haswell's "remarkably black box" (2). In this chapter, I do something similar with style, showing how interiority haunts even that canon's most resolutely social, ecological, and interconnected theories. As in the previous chapter, I argue that this notion is integral rather than incidental to our ways of thinking, talking, and writing about writing. In fact, it is integral to writing itself. In other words, the persistence of these black boxes is not a bug but a feature of writing.

Composition theory should account for this feature, not by adopting more metaphors for writing's relationality—itself another feature of writing, though one that has been explored in detail—but by devising critical language for acknowledging that interiority is functional. By doing so, we might discard the philosophical baggage that burdens our field's considerations of writing, we might put ourselves in a better position to consider Paul Prior's question about "how texts come into being" (172), and we might gain some perspective on the uses of theoretical work in composition studies.

My first step is to examine recent scholarship on style. More than other canons, style focuses unambiguously on the individual writer, and this in turn suggests a way into the idea of interiority, and to an interest in what happens at the moment of a text's creation. More precisely, style underscores the importance of the idea of interiority, and of the idea of something happening at the moment of a text's creation. And its current formulations, which set individual agency against ecological and interconnected scenes of writing, give us a rich framework in which to imagine the theory of identity I have been proposing.

I then conclude this study by returning to invention. But where the previous chapter dealt with works that treat invention as given, here I focus on work that questions its viability. In doing so, I point to a model for theorizing interiority (and therefore identity) as functional. Specifically, I examine John Muckelbauer's *Future of Invention,* which treats invention not as a working concept or theoretical tool but as an ongoing, necessary, and useful problematic. Muckelbauer's study values the canon not because it helps us get at origins but rather because it dramatizes the need for—and the impossibility of—the very idea of origins. Because it does this, *The Future of Invention* helps us think through the problematics of writing and identity that I have been highlighting in this book. But if invention itself becomes the very idea that we examine rather than the conceptual tool with which we examine, then we have to accept that the question of how texts come into being is even more complicated than we might have supposed. Respect for this complication is what I think composition studies must work into its theoretical orientation toward writing.

THE "PROBLEM" OF STYLE

In the introduction to *Performing Prose: The Study and Practice of Style in Composition,* Chris Holcomb and M. Jimmie Killingsworth note the obsolescence of the notion that "a writer's true or authentic self is somehow expressed by . . . the decisions he or she makes at the level of style." They attribute this obsolescence to "changes in how we understand identity." Specifically, contemporary approaches to style emphasize performance. Writers are seen as "playing any number of social roles or showing particular group affiliations." At best, such approaches consider the idea of a "distinctive self" as something expressed "through a singular combination of the conventional selves the writer performs" (27). In addition, Holcomb and Killingsworth point out that contemporary approaches are participatory insofar as writers bring readers into the stylistic performance

(30). According to Holcomb and Killingsworth, these complexities of performance and participation (among others) make style particularly difficult to analyze and practice. The complexities create a "diverse repertoire of stylistic moves—other points of entry into writing and analysis." And, in turn, "each choice and each change has a rippling effect and brings other elements into play" (34).

It is not surprising that a version of complexity applies as well to style as it does to invention. As I have noted, our field's various metaphors of relation are a welcome addition to composition's theoretical, empirical, and pedagogical vocabulary, especially in a time of rapid technological change, expansion, and innovation. But when we take such an approach to style—as I believe we should—we run again, and perhaps more directly, into the same problems of interiority, intention, and agency that present themselves to thinking about invention. Pedagogically, we think of style as the function of an individual's intention, but in our descriptions of writing's scenic complexity—its relationality—intention is distributed. In Chapter 4, I argued that even our most extensively ecological metaphors for invention necessarily maintain a reserve of interiority. And it seems that even the most distributed or contextualized theories of style do the same. But a key difference between invention and style might be that style, as a writing practice, has been seen as something of a black box in its own right. Because of this, its teaching has perhaps been more frankly prescriptive than that of invention, and its theorization has perhaps been less attuned to writing's intricacies and relations.

Rebecca Moore Howard laments this lack of attunement when she notes that "sentence-level pedagogy and scholarship," or style, has not yet developed a "contextualist" sensibility. Howard would like not only to revive style as an area of inquiry but to "transform" it. She would liberate it from the prescriptivist prison in which it has been held by old "textualist methods" represented by the work of such scholars as Joseph Williams. According to Howard, through such a liberation, style would stop being an instrument for the "hegemonic disciplining of students," and it would instead constitute "pedagogical invitations for students to participate in the play of texts" (43).

Howard's approach to style reflects our field's current theoretical understandings of writing, and it informs style's recent rediscovery as a topic of inquiry. Part of this rediscovery, as Howard's critique illustrates, has been the delineation of what style is not, or of what it has been but should no longer be. In addition, other scholars have developed different terms for talking and thinking about style in ways that explicitly break with its textualist and prescriptivist past and move toward a relational future.

For example, in "Style as a System," Drew Loewe argues that past theories of style have tended to cast it as "a set of static properties" adhering to writer, reader, or text that do not account for the canon's "dynamic nature." In their place, he proposes a theory of style as "a system of processes and relationships." Loewe turns to systems theory and cybernetics for "a framework and a vocabulary for describing how, through exchanges of information, members of a system interact with and affect each other dynamically" (241). Such a framework would "account for the reciprocal interrelationships among writers, texts, and audiences," thus providing theorists, researchers, and teachers in the field with a way to approach their objects of study "that does justice to the true complexity (and, indeed, the messiness) of the writing and reading processes" (242). To understand style in this fundamentally relational way is to see it "as a system in which each member of the triad [of writer, audience, and text] affects—and is affected by—the other members" (244).

According to Loewe, this systemic approach helps us avoid applying "a possessory vocabulary" to what are actually relational phenomena (245). Additionally, Loewe finds in cybernetics a salutary reflexivity, one that "foregrounds the role of the observer" (247). This reflexivity helps us understand that our analyses and judgments of style are informed by various and ongoing feedback loops whereby the relationship between observer and observed is mutually transformative. Loewe quotes N. Katherine Hayles to the effect that "we do not see a world 'out there' that exists apart from us. Rather, we see only what our systemic organization allows us to see" (248).

As a consequence, it is possible and necessary to see how "each member of the triad is itself a system with its own internal dynamics," and to see how "each member affects the other members and the 'metasystem' as a whole." In this context, the writing subject becomes a rather complex object of inquiry, one whose relationships to "the rhetorical situation, *kairos,* and embodiment" become objects of inquiry in their own right. This understanding leads Loewe to argue, for example, that Lloyd Bitzer's "three-part taxonomy of exigence, audience, and constraints" requires more fine-grained analysis in order to better describe how the parts of the taxonomy interact (248). Additionally, Loewe cites Jerry Blitefield in order to note that "physical places come in and out of different states of being," which renders them kairotic, and which in turn makes *kairos* "not simply a matter of rhetorical perception or willing agency" but something that writer and audience "define and construct . . . in time and space" (249).

In contrast to Loewe's emphasis on cybernetics and posthumanism, T. R. Johnson applies insights from the work of Gilles Deleuze and like-minded theorists in order to imagine style as something like a surplus or a productive deviation from the transactions that we imagine to compose writing's core function. Drawing also on the work of Brian Massumi, Johnson compares writing to playing a sport, noting that "when someone is playing soccer . . . he or she works not just according to expectations and 'unwritten' rules, but rather plays with and around these to escape codified structure and enter, instead, the realm of creativity, surprise, and intensity." This player, Johnson claims, "is developing a style and working with style as such." Again echoing Massumi, Johnson writes that "to play with style . . . is to toss unregulated intensities into the mix that will charge the game anew, change it, and launch new vectors of becoming." Johnson then extends this idea of deviation to the point where the transactional functions of writing fade into the background, almost disappear. A writer who "works with style," Johnson notes, "does not polish her prose merely to ensure that it will serve as a transparent window onto some extratextual objects. Instead, she has left behind all such tensions between representations and their objects to enter the domain that Gilles Deleuze . . . associates with the simulacrum, a place of dazzling freedom, where possibilities are endlessly put into play, a space that is Dionysian or, in a utopian sense, schizoid." To teach style in this way is to forestall the prospect that students "will struggle with the blank page and complain that they don't have any ideas to write about" (281). This is because "writing, in this sense, is never properly 'about' any particular thing any more than music is. It is writing, in a relatively pure sense, as writing" (281–82).

These examples and others show how the theoretical study of style mirrors developments in other areas of the field. Holcomb and Killingsworth's emphasis on performativity, Howard's interest in contextualism, Loewe's focus on cybernetics and posthumanism, and Johnson's turn to Deleuze all find analogs in theoretical work across composition studies. What they seem to share, however, is an implicit sense that style is a stable or constant epistemological category, one that endures beneath the thematic and theoretical variations that characterize its specific instances. In contrast, I think we have other options for understanding style, options in which we place the category itself under scrutiny and examine its ability to help us think about writing. In these scenarios, we would think of style in terms of the questions I have been raising about interiority. When we do this, we might, for example, find it difficult to maintain a concept of style that is as relational and contextualist as Howard would like while also attending to the idea of singularity that Haswell and Haswell attribute to writers—that is, to the idea that bodies make choices. Such potential contradictions underscore the idea that style is not a transcendent concept, at least not in the way we customarily imagine it to be. Instead, it might be more accurate and useful to say that something called *style* is always part of the scene of writing, but not necessarily a lens through which to contemplate that scene. As part of the scene, style's future becomes unstable, maybe even untenable at times. But this strikes me as a conceptual strength, a potential source of interesting theories of writing and writers—not a problem. From such a perspective, style does not need saving, if by this we mean raising its epistemological value to let it compete with, say, invention.

INVENTION AND STYLE

Still, Paul Butler tries to do precisely this in *Out of Style: Reanimating Stylistic Studies in Composition and Rhetoric*. He claims that the study of style has been relatively neglected until recently, leaving "no recent central body of scholarship . . . that identifies style as a concern in the field." Yet Butler notes that despite its overt neglect, thinking about style is also covertly widespread. So while there are relatively few studies and theories of style that identify themselves as such, we might identify as "stylistic analysis" or "studies in style" a great deal of work that has been carried out in other terms and in various areas of the field. Butler offers reasons for this state of affairs and some explanations for how it came to be. But fundamentally, he believes this approach (or nonapproach) is a distortion of style itself, one that robs composition studies of a potentially rich venue in which to theorize, study, and teach writing. Therefore, he asks the field to develop a richer theory of style, one that pays "greater attention to its dynamic nature and connections to invention, the process movement, and other canons of rhetoric" (22–23). Butler's project, then, is an attempt to make style respectable by likening it to other already-respectable activities in the field.

Style's relation to invention serves as the conceptual core of Butler's work. To him, the best theories of style have always been inventional. Butler wants to reaffirm style's connection to invention so that the former may benefit from the latter's longstanding place of honor in composition studies. This is a political motive, but it also has a legitimate theoretical foundation: invention is our field's most valued canon because it deals with novelty and because, when channeled into pedagogy, it makes the creation of novelty something that can be taught.

In making his case for style's inventiveness, Butler offers a history of its fall from favor. He turns to scholars such as James Zebroski and Louise Wetherbee Phelps, who claim that style is actually a casualty of the field's turn to invention. According to Butler, invention was theorized "as a dynamic aspect of rhetoric" and "in direct contrast to style," which was "perceived to belong, on the other hand, to a static, current-traditional rhetoric" (59). For Butler, a related reason for invention's separation from style is the "longstanding theoretical split between content (that which is invented) and form (style and arrangement)." As Butler puts it, "the debate centers on whether style can be separated from meaning." The belief that it can be separated results in a "dualistic" view, while the contrasting "organic" theory "supports the premise that language and thought necessarily coexist." But despite these debates and distinctions, there were studies that "viewed style and invention as connected in dynamic ways" and "not as part of the current-traditional rhetoric with which style has often been negatively associated" (61). That is, an idea of inventional style existed, and continues to exist, based as it is on the canon's "unique ability . . . to facilitate the invention of ideas through writing." Along these lines, certain scholars asserted the unity, or at least the connectedness, of the two canons. As examples, he points to a 1970 statement by the NCTE Committee on the Nature of Rhetorical Invention, John Gage's "Philosophies of Style" essay in *College English* (1980), Ross Winterowd's *Contemporary Rhetoric* (1975), and, perhaps most important, Richard Young, Alton Becker, and Kenneth Pike's *Rhetoric: Discovery and Change* (1970).

According to Butler, in the 1970s Young, Becker, and Pike were the most forceful advocates of an inventive style. Young and Becker had developed this theory in the late 1960s through the more general concept of "the universe of discourse" (70). The resulting textbook, written with Pike, *Rhetoric: Discovery and Change,* redefined style with an "emphasis on epistemological implications." It "proposed a new view of the writer as a 'creator' who 'must see the art of rhetoric in dynamic terms, as search and choice, as a way of behaving.'" Butler notes that "their view of style as social, rhetorical, and inventional suggested its close affiliation with today's popular conceptions of the process of writing" (71).

Butler cites Richard Lanham as another scholar for whom style has inventional properties. In *Style: An Anti-Textbook*, Lanham acknowledges that invention and arrangement are usually at the center of writing courses, but he notes that "both, implicit in a study of style, emerge naturally only from a concentration on it"

(13–14). According to Butler, Lanham believes "it is important to look self-consciously *at* the stylistic surface—what he called the opaque style—rather than *through* style to an underlying reality where a transparent content is normally thought to exist" (75). In fact, according to Butler, Lanham "is perhaps one of the only recent scholars to assume that style is *the* indispensable rhetorical canon that cannot be ignored" (76).

Similarly, says Butler, Francis Christensen emphasizes syntax and stresses "the cognitive importance of being able to articulate relationships among concepts and phenomena," thus promoting an inventional conception of style (77–78). His idea of the cumulative sentence "allows the writer to express more complex ideas and relationships, which is what makes writing 'better' or more mature" (78). According to Butler, Christensen's cumulative sentence, "with its principle of addition that involves right-branching and left-branching sentences," prompts or forces invention insofar as it requires a writer to "explore the implications of an idea" (79). Thus "the very form of the sentence" serves as a method of invention (79). Butler turns as well to sentence combining, seeing it as a strategy that, like generative rhetoric, aimed at "syntactic maturity" and was, thereby, an inventional approach to style. Of course, there are key differences between the two. The latter "is based on structural grammar," while the former "originates in Chomsky's transformational-generative grammar" (80). Generative grammar emphasizes "principles of addition, direction of modification, levels of generality, and texture," whereas sentence combining "uses techniques of embedding, deletion, subordination, and coordination" (80). Butler claims that "if it is true, as Chomsky argued, that the deep structures (relational patterns) of a language can generate an indefinite number of understandable statements (surface structures), then the very act of choosing among—or generating choice among—numerous possibilities itself involves an inventive process, that is, a process of choice and creation" (80–81).

Like the other theorists I have discussed in this chapter, Butler's inventional style is a stable concept, a tool with which to think and teach. Its fortunes may vary, as various scholars write various theories and conduct various studies about it, but there remains an entity called *style* that everyone agrees exists and is useful for the study and teaching of writing. But of course, its continued use—our disciplinary agreement to keep thinking about it, even if to downplay or disparage it—is what gives style its apparent stability. Butler contributes to style's stability merely by writing a book about it. Of course, he takes many more steps than this, gathering and generating statements about style that argue for its inventional capacity.

But if style is "as good as" invention, then it is also as problematic as invention, and for similar reasons. Butler argues that style, recognized in its proper complexity, gives composition studies more and better equipment for doing its work, and he is certainly right about this. And comparing style and invention makes a great deal of sense. But in doing so, I fear we risk overlooking some of style's unique strengths, especially as they relate to our ability to theorize the interiority that relational theories of invention seem to take for granted—the same interiority that I claim is built-in to writing itself.

In a way, I am suggesting that style is a less philosophical canon than invention, a point suggested by Butler's own survey and analysis of the field. Even when we theorize style as supremely relational—as we should—we still understand it to be a matter of individual choices. These may be embedded in contexts whose complexity we may struggle to map and understand, but we still understand them as choices, as individual decisions—however overdetermined. And this is extremely useful. Because style's emphasis on the individual is intense and focused, it is uniquely suited (among the rhetorical canons, at least) to a discussion of the interiority and identity that—I have argued—attaches to the individual. Style gives us permission to sidestep the false subject/object dualism of modern philosophy while retaining the concept of novelty. But the novelty generated through style is contingent, even ephemeral, and the interiority it suggests is temporary and elusive. This interiority is no less functional because of this; in fact, it might even be more so.

THE INVENTION-EFFECT

But, ironically, a book-length study of invention is what points a way to such an approach. Muckelbauer's *Future of Invention* is an extended meditation on the possibility and viability of that canon. It never discards invention, of course, but neither is it entirely comfortable with the idea. Instead, Muckelbauer theorizes, speculates, and muses about the canon on the way to developing a new orientation toward it. For reasons I make clear below, he does not offer a new theory of invention. Rather, he proposes a new way for theorists to think about the idea, uses, and functions of invention.

First, and most important, Muckelbauer wants to liberate invention from the clutches of dialectic. By *dialectic* I take him to mean not only a method of philosophical discussion (and the counterpart of rhetoric) but also, more generally, a philosophical disposition. That is, he wants to cast invention "in a register that is irreducible to dialectical repetition" in order to avoid the agonistic process that he sees characterizing most inventional theories (38). According to this agonistic process, "difference and novelty only emerge by somehow overcoming or negating particular others" (4). Negation involves reduction, stasis, and the taking of positions, which can in turn be attacked, defended, modified, synthesized, or otherwise managed. At the same time, however, Muckelbauer acknowledges that the idea of abandoning dialectic is problematic; in the end, the attempt to break away from dialectic is itself a dialectical act, which means that "the structure of negative relations stays the same" (11). This paradox pervades Muckelbauer's text, and in doing so, it does him the favor of highlighting the problem's complexity.

Nonetheless, Muckelbauer tries to get out of the paradox by seeking an "affirmative" image of change or novelty. Toward this end, and following the work of Deleuze, he points to the idea that there are "singular rhythms," which he likens to what are called "moments of insight," "inspiration," or "creativity" (34). These rhythms emerge from dialectic's negation, but they do so despite dialectic's drive to manage, control, and direct change through logic, claims, proof, and argumentation. They escape from the signifying content that dialectic creates, preserves, and repeats. And in doing so, they speak to the idea that "arguments and claims may well be the least interesting dimension of writing, despite the fact that they remain invaluable" (42). They indicate that there is more to writing and rhetoric than the substance of any particular claim made through writing and rhetoric. In other words, the term *singular rhythms* names the unpredictable, unexpected dimensions of any discursive activity. It points to the idea that something occurs in discourse that does not participate in representation but nonetheless exists alongside it. Dialectic may be pervasive and unavoidable, but it is also incomplete and inefficient. It generates rhetorical remainders, outliers, or excesses that representation does not or cannot accommodate. Representation—the domain that dialectical processes such as critique and synthesis authorize—is not the sum total of communication. And what remains or escapes as a result of dialectic's incompleteness is "affirmative" to the extent that it is not part of dialectic's usual back-and-forth, give-and-take.

According to Muckelbauer, rhetorical theory provides an "extremely productive site through which [to] explain this affirmative sense of change." Rhetoric already understands that communication exceeds representation. Its "traditional concern for persuasion" has led it to address "questions of force rather than questions of signification or meaning," to attend to "the dimension of language that is irreducible to questions of meaning and understanding" (13). Its concern with persuasion orients rhetoric toward discourse's "capacity to exert a compelling force, its ability to evoke particular responses in specific audiences" (17). Persuasion, according to Muckelbauer, "is not primarily concerned with understanding or *even with the effort to prevent misunderstanding.*" As a result, "the fact that meaning might turn out to be indeterminate or structurally incomplete . . . is really not of very much consequence" (18). Moreover, relatively recent rhetorical theories make even stronger claims, proposing "a generalized art of invention, an architectonic rubric for all modes of inquiry," that is, a generative rhetoric (21). Yet Muckelbauer notes that despite this antifoundational orientation, rhetoric seems resolutely foundational on the question of "the status of the subject" (26). Scholars of rhetoric have balked at applying the same contingency and contextuality to subjects that they afford to objects (26). Indeed, according to Muckelbauer, "scholarship in rhetoric remains deeply committed to what is generally referred to as a 'humanist' model of subjectivity—a model that tends to emphasize the primary importance of categories such as consciousness, identity, and agency" (26). As a result, rhetorical theory maintains invention as an intentional activity, something that a subject does and controls. Even the most forward-looking conceptions of invention maintain Platonic-Aristotelian orientations toward knowledge production. For Muckelbauer, such notions of invention are "fundamentally appropriative," engaged in "an effort to master the unknown by transforming it into knowledge" (29). So, dialectic endures, and rhetoric misses its opportunity to think invention differently.

But rhetorical theory is not alone: postmodern critique does the same thing when it turns into what Muckelbauer calls "an instrumental methodology" (32). Postmodern critiques "advance themselves as a position, as a content that locates itself in relation to some other position." Therefore, they "cannot help but partake of the logic of identity and the dialectical movement of appropriation that it enables" (32). According to Muckelbauer, this adherence to dialectic—by both rhetoric and postmodern critique—"is why the humanism vs. postmodernism debate truly is as endless as it seems, and why the impasse of this debate is tiresome and frustrating" (32–33). So it seems that no one can avoid dialectic (not even Muckelbauer himself, as he readily admits). This is why the task at hand is more complicated than devising a new theory of invention. And yet, neither can we simply dispense with invention. Invention embodies the idea of a relation between old and new—a useful and even necessary feature for thinking about how texts come into being. Specifically, invention involves offering "a concept of the future that presents itself as a decisive break from the past," and even though the substance of this concept is called into question (and rightly so) by Muckelbauer, the function of this concept is what most interests me.

If invention is a vehicle for enacting a relationship between old and new, then the idea of tradition is crucial as well. It is a vehicle for imagining a past. For Muckelbauer, tradition "not only orders a series of past actions, but also demands that they be repeated" (144). But, again, if "the only way to introduce something different" is to "transgress" or "negate" (i.e., to break with tradition), then the core of rhetorical invention continues to be negation, that is, dialectic. Yet Muckelbauer works around this problem by claiming that it is difficult, even untenable, to differentiate between tradition and innovation. This is because "a future that is not merely a repetition of the same requires an engagement with tradition that is something other than a simple refusal or an absolute break" (146). Mere negation is not a workable concept. Instead, there is another paradox (or another version of the paradox I mentioned above). It is identified as such by Derrida, whom Muckelbauer summarizes: on the one hand, truly innovative invention "must be so extraordinary as to exceed even the possibility of its own reception" (147). On the other hand, as Derrida himself states, "Invention is invented only if repetition, generality, common availability, and thus publicity are introduced or promised in the structure of the first time" ("Psyche" 34). In other words, and strictly speaking, invention does not work, at least not as we usually imagine it to work in our theories and pedagogies. The very idea of *old/new* (or *tradition/innovation*) is overwhelmed by conceptual difficulties. But we do not need for invention to work conceptually; for our purposes, it will do for invention to work functionally. An invention-effect would be more useful, and more appropriate, as it would name the feature of writing that mobilizes writing—that allows writing to proceed as if it made sense to speak of its beginnings. The question of where texts come from is one that we cannot answer empirically, and yet it is one we are compelled to ask. And the thing that compels us to ask it is the structure of writing itself.

CONCLUSION

As I have argued, the metaphors of relation we use to describe writing's entwinement in the world cannot help us answer the question of where texts come from. Neither can they help us know what goes on in individual acts of writing, within Haswell and Haswell's "remarkably black box." And because we cannot answer the question empirically, we might be tempted to abandon it. I would not, and my reasons have as much to do with getting at the truth about writing as they do with how we go about trying to get at the truth about writing. That is, my concerns are methodological. For those of us who work in the theoretical corners of our field, who spend time and effort thinking about how best to think about writing, it is good to remember that even the most seemingly esoteric work has practical implications. By practical, I don't necessarily refer to classroom application or even research design—though I would not rule them out. I mean our attitudes, in the Burkean sense, toward our objects of inquiry: writers, acts of writing, and writing itself. I think few would disagree that it is practical—that is to say intellectually useful—for a field to have its fundamental suppositions regularly questioned and, when found inadequate, revised or overturned.

For that matter, it is practical and necessary to identify a field's new suppositions: those beliefs or assumptions that have become blackboxed (to borrow from Bruno Latour in *Science in Action*) or that have been encrypted into god-terms (to borrow again from Burke). In fact, I take as a methodological principle the idea that such boxes or terms should be the object of *constant* theoretical inquiry. The theoretical study of writing is, as I see it, an unending search for black boxes and god-terms, a constant destabilizing of every patch of ground in our field, in order to keep the field honest, as it were. The methodology I am describing sees composition studies not as an advancing field; it does not necessarily imagine an accretion of knowledge about acts of writing, writing subjects, and writing. If anything, I am describing a theoretical method whereby we constantly remind ourselves that we do not and cannot move forward in any conventional sense.

Toward that end, and in this book, I have asked us to think of exteriority and interiority as functions of writing, rather than features of the world as such. I have asked us to use *event* as a handy term for describing the encounter between the functions of exteriority and interiority, and I have proposed *identity* as a term for describing that encounter as it is said to take place at moments of inscription. What I like about these terms is the way they try to extend the discursive and symbolic complexities that surround writers and writing subjects "into" writers and writing subjects. Other terms might do a similar and even better job. But the issue is less our choice of particular terms than how we, as scholars and teachers of writing, engage them. In other words, I have not been trying to say something new about writing. I have, instead, been trying to say something new about what we say—and how we think—about writing.

WORKS CITED

Alcoff, Linda Martín. "Who's Afraid of Identity Politics?" Moya and Hames-García 312–44. Print.
Anderson, Dana. *Identity's Strategy: Rhetorical Selves in Conversion*. Columbia: South Carolina UP, 2007. Print.
Atkins, G. Douglas, and Michael L. Johnson, eds. *Writing and Reading Differently: Deconstruction and the Teaching of Composition and Literature*. Lawrence: UP of Kansas, 1985. Print.
Badiou, Alain. *Ethics: An Essay on the Understanding of Evil*. Trans. Peter Hallward. New York: Verso, 2001. Print.
———. *Logics of Worlds: Being and Event, 2*. Trans. Alberto Toscano. New York: Continuum, 2009. Print.
Ball, Arnetha F., and Pamela Ellis. "Identity and the Writing of Culturally and Linguistically Diverse Students." *Handbook of Research on Writing: History, Society, School, Individual, Text*. Ed. Charles Bazerman. New York: Erlbaum, 2008. 499–513. Print.
Ball, Arnetha F., and Ted Lardner. *African American Literacies Unleashed: Vernacular English and the Composition Classroom*. Carbondale: Southern Illinois UP, 2005. Print.
Ballif, Michelle. *Seduction, Sophistry, and the Woman with the Rhetorical Figure*. Carbondale: Southern Illinois UP, 2001. Print.
Bawarshi, Anis. *Genre and the Invention of the Writer: Reconsidering the Place of Invention in Composition*. Logan: Utah State UP, 2003.
Bazerman, Charles, and Paul Prior, eds. *What Writing Does and How It Does It: An Introduction to Analyzing Texts and Textual Practices*. Mahwah: Erlbaum, 2004. Print.
Berkenkotter, Carol. "The Legacy of Positivism in Empirical Composition Research." *JAC* 9 (1989): 69–82. Web. 3 Mar. 2017.
Berlin, James. "Rhetoric and Ideology in the Writing Class." *College English* 50.5 (1988): 477–94. *JSTOR*. Web. 8 Mar. 2017. www.jstor.org/stable/377477.

Berthoff, Ann E. "Learning the Uses of Chaos." Freedman and Pringle 75–78. Print.

Bolter, Jay David. *Writing Space: The Computer, Hypertext, and the History of Writing.* Hillsdale: Erlbaum, 1991. Print.

Britton, James. "Shaping at the Point of Utterance." Freedman and Pringle 61–65. Print.

Brooke, Collin Gifford. *Lingua Fracta: Towards a Rhetoric of New Media.* Cresskill: Hampton, 2009. Print.

Burgess, Amy, and Roz Ivanič. "Writing and Being Written: Issues of Identity Across Timescales." *Written Communication* 27.2 (2010): 228–55. *Sage Journals Online.* Web. 6 Mar. 2017. DOI: 10.1177/0741088310363447.

Burke, Kenneth. *A Grammar of Motives.* 1945. Berkeley: U of California P, 1969. Print.

———. *Language as Symbolic Action: Essays on Life, Literature, and Method.* Berkeley: U of California P, 1966. Print.

———. *A Rhetoric of Motives.* 1950. Rev. ed. Berkeley: U of California P, 1969. Print.

Butler, Judith. *Gender Trouble: Feminism and the Subversion of Identity.* New York: Routledge, 1990. Print.

———. *The Psychic Life of Power: Theories in Subjection.* Stanford: Stanford UP, 1997. Print.

Butler, Paul. *Out of Style: Reanimating Stylistic Study in Composition and Rhetoric.* Logan: Utah State UP, 2008. *Project Muse.* Web. 28 Mar. 2017.

Castells, Manuel. *The Power of Identity,* 2d ed. Malden: Blackwell, 2004. Print.

Cooper, Marilyn M. "Nonessentialist Identity and the National Discourse." *Rhetoric and Ethnicity.* Ed. Keith Gilyard and Vorris Nunley. Portsmouth: Heinemann, 2004. 87–102. Print.

Cox, Michelle, Jay Jordan, Christina Ortmeier-Hooper, and Gwen Gray Schwartz. Introduction. Cox et al. xv–xxviii. Print.

———, eds. *Reinventing Identities in Second Language Writing.* Urbana, IL: NCTE, 2010. Print.

Crowley, Sharon. "Body Studies in Rhetoric and Composition." *Rhetoric and Composition as Intellectual Work.* Ed. Gary A. Olson. Carbondale: Southern Illinois UP, 2002. 177–87. Print.

———. *The Methodical Memory: Invention in Current-Traditional Rhetoric.* 1990. Carbondale: Southern Illinois UP, 2010. Print.

Crusius, Timothy W. "A Case for Burke's Dialectic and Rhetoric." *Philosophy and Rhetoric* 19.1 (1986): 23–37. *EBSCOhost.* Web. 6 Mar. 2017.

Dasenbrock, Reed Way. "Becoming Aware of the Myth of Presence." *JAC* 8 (1988): 1–11. Web. 6 Mar. 2017.

Davis, D. Diane. *Breaking Up [at] Totality: A Rhetoric of Laughter*. Carbondale: Southern Illinois UP, 2000. Print.

Day, Ronald E. *The Modern Invention of Information: Discourse, History, and Power*. Carbondale: Southern Illinois UP, 2001. Print.

Deleuze, Gilles. *Bergsonism*. Trans. Hugh Tomlinson and Barbara Habberjam. New York: Zone, 1991. Print.

———. *Difference and Repetition*. Trans. Paul Patton. New York: Columbia UP, 1994. Print.

———. *The Logic of Sense*. Trans. Mark Lester with Charles Stivale. New York: Continuum, 2004. Print.

Derrida, Jacques. "A Certain Impossible Possibility of Saying the Event." Trans. Gila Walker. *Critical Inquiry* 33.2 (2007): 441–61. *JSTOR*. Web. 6 Mar. 2017. DOI: 10.1086/511506.

———. "The Deaths of Roland Barthes." Trans. Pascale-Anne Brault and Michael Naas. *Psyche: Inventions of the Other.*Vol.1. 264–98. Print.

———. *Of Grammatology*. Corrected ed. Trans. Gayatri Chakravorty Spivak. Baltimore: Johns Hopkins UP, 1997. Print.

———. "Psyche: Invention of the Other." Trans. Catherine Porter. *Psyche: Inventions of the Other.* Vol. 1. 1–47. Print.

———. *Psyche: Inventions of the Other*. Ed. Peggy Kamuf and Elizabeth Rottenberg. 2 vols. Stanford: Stanford UP, 2007. Print.

———. "Signature Event Context." *Margins of Philosophy*. Trans. Alan Bass. Chicago: U of Chicago P, 1982. 307–30. Print.

Durst, Russel K. "Writing at the Postsecondary Level." *Research on Composition: Multiple Perspectives on Two Decades of Change*. Ed. Peter Smagorinsky. New York: Teachers College P, 2006. 78–107. Print.

Emig, Janet A. *The Composing Processes of Twelfth Graders*. Urbana: NCTE, 1971. Print.

Faigley, Lester. *Fragments of Rationality: Postmodernity and the Subject of Composition*. Pittsburgh: U of Pittsburgh P, 1992. Print.

Flower, Linda. *The Construction of Negotiated Meaning: A Social Cognitive Theory of Writing*. Carbondale: Southern Illinois UP, 1994. Print.

———. "Observation-Based Theory Building." *Publishing in Rhetoric and Composition*. Ed. Gary A. Olson and Todd W. Taylor. Albany: State U of New York P, 1997. 163–85. Print.

Flower, Linda, and John R. Hayes. "The Cognition of Discovery: Defining a Rhetorical Problem." *College Composition and Communication* 31.1 (1980): 21–32. *JSTOR*. Web. 16 Mar. 2017. www.jstor.org/stable/356630.

———. "A Cognitive Process Theory of Writing." *College Composition and Communication* 32.4 (1981): 365–87. *JSTOR*. Web. 16 Mar. 2017. www.jstor.org/stable/356600.

Foster, David. "What Are We Talking about When We Talk about Composition?" *JAC* 8 (1988): 30–40. Web. 8 Mar. 2017.

Freedman, Aviva, and Ian Pringle, eds. *Reinventing the Rhetorical Tradition*. Ottawa: Canadian Council of Teachers of English, 1980. Print.

Gilyard, Keith. "Literacy, Identity, Imagination, Flight." *College Composition and Communication* 52.2 (2000): 260–72. *ProQuest*. Web. 6 Mar. 2017.

Gonçalves, Zan Meyer. *Sexuality and the Politics of Ethos in the Writing Classroom*. Carbondale: Southern Illinois UP, 2005. Print.

Hall, Stuart. "Introduction: Who Needs 'Identity?'" *Questions of Cultural Identity*. Ed. Stuart Hall and Paul du Gay. London: Sage, 1996. 1–17. Print.

Hansen, Mark. *Embodying Technesis: Technology beyond Writing*. Ann Arbor: U of Michigan P, 2000. Print.

Haswell, Janis, and Richard Haswell. *Authoring: An Essay for the English Profession on Potentiality and Singularity*. Logan: Utah State UP, 2010. Print.

Hawk, Byron. *A Counter-History of Composition: Toward Methodologies of Complexity*. Pittsburgh: U of Pittsburgh P, 2007. Print.

Hayles, N. Katherine. *How We Became Posthuman: Virtual Bodies in Cybernetics, Literature, and Informatics*. Chicago: U of Chicago P, 1999. Print.

Hegeman, Susan. *The Cultural Return*. Berkeley: U of California P, 2012. Print.

Holcomb, Chris, and M. Jimmie Killingsworth. *Performing Prose: The Study and Practice of Style in Composition*. Carbondale: Southern Illinois UP, 2010. Print.

Howard, Rebecca Moore. "Contextualist Stylistics: Breaking Down the Binaries in Sentence-Level Pedagogy." Johnson and Pace 42–56. Print.

Johnson, T. R. "Writing with the Ear." Johnson and Pace 267–85. Print.

Johnson, T. R., and Tom Pace, eds. *Refiguring Prose Style: Possibilities for Writing Pedagogy*. Logan: Utah State UP, 2005. Print.

Kamberelis, George, and Lenora de la Luna. "Children's Writing: How Textual Forms, Contextual Forces, and Textual Politics Co-Emerge." Bazerman and Prior 239–78. Print.

Kill, Melanie. "Acknowledging the Rough Edges of Resistance: Negotiation of Identities for First-Year Composition." *College Composition and Communication* 58.2 (2006): 213–35. *ProQuest*. Web. 6 Mar. 2017.

Landow, George P. *Hypertext: The Convergence of Contemporary Critical Theory and Technology.* Baltimore: Johns Hopkins UP, 1992. Print.

Lanham, Richard A. *Literacy and the Survival of Humanism.* New Haven: Yale UP, 1983. Print.

———. *Style: An Anti-Textbook.* New Haven: Yale UP, 1974. Print.

Latour, Bruno. *Reassembling the Social: An Introduction to Actor-Network-Theory.* New York: Oxford UP, 2005. Print.

———. *Science in Action: How to Follow Scientists and Engineers through Society.* Cambridge: Harvard UP, 1987. Print.

Lauer, Janice M. *Invention in Rhetoric and Composition.* West Lafayette: Parlor Press and the WAC Clearinghouse, 2004. Web. 28 Mar. 2017.

LeCourt, Donna. *Identity Matters: Schooling the Student Body in Academic Discourse.* Albany: State U of New York P, 2004. Print.

LeFevre, Karen Burke. *Invention as a Social Act.* Carbondale: Southern Illinois UP, 1987. Print.

Loewe, Drew. "Style as a System: Toward a Cybernetic Model of Composition Style." Johnson and Pace 241–55. Print.

McComiskey, Bruce. Rev. of *Literacy Matters: Writing and Reading the Social Self,* by Robert P. Yagelski. *College Composition and Communication* 53.4 (2002): 751–54. *ProQuest.* Web. 6 Mar. 2017.

Meillassoux, Quentin. *After Finitude: An Essay on the Necessity of Contingency.* Trans. Ray Brassier. London: Continuum, 2009. Print.

Mejía, Jaime Armin. "Arts of the U.S.–Mexico Contact Zone." *Crossing Borderlands: Composition and Postcolonial Studies.* Ed. Andrea A. Lunsford and Lahoucine Ouzgane. Pittsburgh: U of Pittsburgh P, 2004. 171–98. Print.

Michaels, Walter Benn. *Our America: Nativism, Modernism, and Pluralism.* Durham: Duke UP, 1995. Print.

Miller, Susan. *Assuming the Positions: Cultural Pedagogy and the Politics of Commonplace Writing.* Pittsburgh: U of Pittsburgh P, 1998. Print.

———. *Rescuing the Subject: A Critical Introduction to Rhetoric and the Writer.* 1989. Carbondale: Southern Illinois UP, 2004. Print.

———. *Trust in Texts: A Different History of Rhetoric.* Carbondale: Southern Illinois UP, 2008. Print.

Mohanty, Satya P. "The Epistemic Status of Cultural Identity: On *Beloved* and the Postcolonial Condition." *Cultural Critique* 24 (1993): 41–80. *JSTOR.* Web. 28 Mar. 2017. DOI: 10.2307/1354129. Rpt. in Moya and Hames-García 29–66. Print.

Moya, Paula M. L., and Michael R. Hames-García, eds. *Reclaiming Identity: Realist Theory and the Predicament of Postmodernism.* Berkeley: U of California P, 2000. Print.

Muckelbauer, John. *The Future of Invention: Rhetoric, Postmodernism, and the Problem of Change.* Albany: State U of New York P, 2008. Print.

Murray, Donald. "Writing as Process: How Writing Finds Its Own Meaning." *The Essential Don Murray: Lessons from America's Greatest Writing Teacher.* Ed. Thomas Newkirk and Lisa C. Miller. Portsmouth: Boynton/Cook, 2009. 6–26. Print.

Neel, Jasper. *Plato, Derrida, and Writing.* Carbondale: Southern Illinois UP, 1988. Print.

Newkirk, Thomas. *The Performance of Self in Student Writing.* Portsmouth: Boynton/Cook, 1997. Print.

Pedersen, Anne-Marie. "Negotiating Cultural Identities through Language: Academic English in Jordan." *College Composition and Communication* 62.2 (2010): 283–310. *ProQuest.* Web. 6 Mar. 2017.

Prior, Paul. "Tracing Process: How Texts Come into Being." Bazerman and Prior 167–200. Print.

Readings, Bill. *Introducing Lyotard: Art and Politics.* New York: Routledge, 1991. Print.

Reid, Alexander. *The Two Virtuals: New Media and Composition.* West Lafayette: Parlor, 2007. *ProQuest.* Web. 28 Mar. 2017.

Rickert, Thomas. *Acts of Enjoyment: Rhetoric, Žižek, and the Return of the Subject.* Pittsburgh: U of Pittsburgh P, 2007. Print.

———. *Ambient Rhetoric: The Attunements of Rhetorical Being.* Pittsburgh: U of Pittsburgh P, 2013. Print.

Rorty, Richard. *Philosophy and the Mirror of Nature.* Princeton: Princeton UP, 1979. Print.

Sánchez, Raúl. *The Function of Theory in Composition Studies.* Albany: State U of New York P, 2005. Print.

Schilb, John. "Ideology and Composition Scholarship." *JAC* 8 (1988): 22–29. Web. 28 Mar. 2017.

———. "The Ideology of 'Epistemological Ecumenicalism': A Response to Carol Berkenkotter." *JAC* 10 (1990): 153–56. Web. 28 Mar. 2017.

Shuck, Gail. "Language Identity, Agency, and Context: The Shifting Meanings of *Multilingual.*" Cox et al. 117–38. Print.

Terranova, Tiziana. *Network Culture: Politics for the Information Age.* Ann Arbor: Pluto, 2004. *EBSCOhost.* Web. 28 Mar. 2017.

Ulmer, Gregory L. *Electronic Monuments.* Minneapolis: U of Minnesota P, 2005. Print.

———. *Heuretics: The Logic of Invention.* Baltimore: Johns Hopkins UP, 1994. Print.

———. "Textshop for Post(e)pedagogy." *Writing and Reading Differently: Deconstruction and the Teaching of Composition and Literature.* Ed. G.

Douglas Atkins and Michael L. Johnson. Lawrence: UP of Kansas, 1985. 38–64. Print.

Vitanza, Victor J. "Critical Sub/Versions of the History of Philosophical Rhetoric." *Rhetoric Review* 6.1 (1987): 41–66. *JSTOR*. Web. 28 Mar. 2017. www.jstor.org/stable/465949.

———. *Negation, Subjectivity, and the History of Rhetoric*. Albany: State U of New York P, 1997. Print.

Wegner, Phillip E. *Life between Two Deaths, 1989–2001: U.S. Culture in the Long Nineties*. Durham: Duke UP, 2009. Print.

Weisser, Christian R. "Ecocomposition and the Greening of Identity." *Ecocomposition: Theoretical and Pedagogical Approaches*. Ed. Weisser and Sidney I. Dobrin. Albany: State U of New York P, 2001. 81–95. Print.

Williams, Bronwyn T, ed. *Identity Papers: Literacy and Power in Higher Education*. Logan: Utah State UP, 2006. Print.

———. Introduction: Literacy, Power, and the Shaping of Identity. Williams 1–13. Print.

Worsham, Lynn. "Composing (Identity) in a Posttraumatic Age." Williams 170–81. Print.

Yagelski, Robert P. *Literacy Matters: Writing and Reading the Social Self*. New York: Teachers College P, 2000. Print.

———. *Writing as a Way of Being: Writing Instruction, Nonduality, and the Crisis of Sustainability*. New York: Hampton, 2011. Print.

INDEX

Agency. *See also* Identity
  and authorship, 43–45
  and consciousness, 72
  Derrida on, 71
  as object of inquiry, 39–40
  of writers, 10, 14, 79–80
Alcoff, Linda Martin, 13, 35–36
Anderson, Dana, 16–17
  Identity's Strategy: Rhetorical Selves in Conversion, 65–69
Atkins, G. Douglas, 47
Authorship, 43–45

Badiou, Alain, 12, 69
Ball, Arnetha, 62
Ballif, Michelle, 59, 60
Barthes, Roland, 6, 83
Bawarshi, Anis, 83
  Genre and the Invention of the Writer, 79–81
Bergson, Henri, 42, 65
Berkenkotter, Carol, 19, 24
Berlin, James, 2, 23
Berthoff, Ann, 7
Bitzer, Lloyd, 102
Blitefield, Jerry, 102
Bolter, Jay David, 43
Britton, James, 3, 7
Brooke, Collin Gifford, 43, 44, 45, 82–84
Burgess, Amy, 62
Burke, Kenneth, 7, 8, 16, 26, 30, 96
  on identity, 67–68
Butler, Judith, 16, 57

Butler, Paul, 18
  Out of Style: Reanimating Stylistic Studies in Composition and Rhetoric, 18, 104–7

Castells, Manuel, 11
Chora, 91–94
Christensen, Francis, 106
Circulation, writing as, 52–56
Cognition
  and consciousness, 41–43
  distributed, 41
  Flower and Hayes model of, 40–41
Communication, writing as, 46–48
Composition, vs. inscription, 3
Composition studies
  focus of, 20
  identity in, 59–61
  and materiality, 81
  and postmodernism, 23–28
  and writerly agency, 39–40
Conduit model, 48
Cooper, Marilyn, 61
Cox, Michelle, 62
Crowley, Sharon, 27
Crusius, Timothy, 67

Dasenbrock, Reed Way, 47
Davis, Diane, 59, 60
Day, Ronald E., 48
Deconstructionism, and exteriority, 4–5
Deleuze, Gilles, 12, 65, 90–91, 102
Deleuzean theory, 42

Derrida, Jacques, 17, 20
    on agency, 71
    on event concept, 69–71
    on invention, 111
    on iterability, 39
    on *punctum*, 5–6
    on signified as elusive, 8
    on *studium*, 6
Dialectical terms, 30
Dialectic, 65–68, 108–9
Distributed cognition, 41
Distribution, 83
Durst, Russel, 1

Ellis, Pamela, 62
Embodiment. *See also* Materiality
    Crowley on, 27
    Hawk on, 88–89
    Hayles on, 31–33
    and student writers, 16, 63–65
Emig, Janet, 20
Empiricism, 23–27
Epistemology, 35–36
Essentialism, 27–28
Event. *See also* Identity
    Badiou on, 69
    definitions of, 12
    Derrida on, 69–71
    exteriority of, 69, 72
    identity as, 13, 72–73
    of writing, 12–13
Exteriority
    and deconstructionism, 4–5
    as dependent on interiority, 6
    essentialism of, 13
    of the event, 69, 72
    Hansen on, 29–31
    materiality as, 31
    overview of, 4–6
    and postmodernism, 23
    terminology of, 9
    of writing, 7–9

Faigley, Lester, 21, 23
Flower, Linda, 25, 40–41

Genres, of invention, 79–82
Gilyard, Keith, 63
Gonçalves, Zan Meyer, 60
Grosz, Elizabeth, 32

Hall, Stuart, 16, 34, 37, 57, 64
Hansen, Mark, 13
    Embodying Technesis: Technology beyond Writing, 28–31
    on exteriority, 29–31
    on language, 30–31
Haswell, Janis, 1–2, 17–18
Haswell, Richard, 1–2, 17–18
Hawk, Byron, *A Counter-History of Composition*, 86–91
Hayes, John, 40–41
Hayles, N. Katherine, 13
    on code, 49
    on embodiment, 31–32
    How We Became Posthuman, 31–32
Hegeman, Susan, 9
Hermeneutics, 83
Holcomb, Chris, *Performing Prose: The Study and Practice of Style in Composition*, 99–100
Howard, Rebecca Moore, 100–101
Hypertext criticism, 43–44

Identity. *See also* Agency
    Anderson on, 65–69
    Burke on, 67–68
    in composition studies, 59–61
    definitions of, 9
    as event, 13, 72–73
    event-based theory of, 15, 17–18, 38
    as fluid, 61–65
    Hall on, 57, 64
    vs. identities, 15
    as performative, 16, 57–58, 66
    and poststructuralism, 9–10
    as strategy, 65–69
    theories of, 34–37, 59–61
    value of, 11
Identity-as-concept, 60

Information, writing as, 48–52
Inscription, vs. composition, 3
Interiority
   as dependent on exteriority, 6
   and invention, 96–97
   and style, 98–99
Invention
   Brooke on, 82–84
   defined, 79
   Derrida on, 111
   ecological model of, 80, 82
   genres of, 79–82
   Hawk on, 86–91
   and interiority, 96–97
   Muckelbauer on, 108–11
   Murray on, 84–85
   and novelty, 76–78
   Rickert on, 91–95
   and style, 100, 104–7
   theories of, 17, 75–76
Iterability, defined, 39
Ivanič, Roz, 62

Johnson, Michael L., 47
Johnson, T. R., 102
Jordan, Jay, 62

Kamberelis, George, 41
Kameen, Paul, 87
Kill, Melanie, 62
Killingsworth, M. Jimmie, *Performing Prose: The Study and Practice of Style in Composition*, 99–100

Landow, George, 43–44
Language, 30–31
Lanham, Richard, 3, 105–6
Lardner, Ted, 62
Latour, Bruno, 24, 25
Lauer, Janice, 77
LeCourt, Donna, 16
   Identity Matters: Schooling the Student Body in Academic Discourse, 63–65
LeFevre, Karen Burke, 80, 82–83

Loewe, Drew, "Style as a System," 101–2
Luna, Lenora de la, 41

Massumi, Brian, 102
Materiality. *See also* Embodiment
   and composition studies, 81
   as exteriority, 31
   of technology, 29–30
   as ultimate vs. dialectical term, 30
McCloskey, Deirdre, 68
McComiskey, Bruce, 2
Meillassoux, Quentin, 69
Mejía, Jaime Armin, 61
Miller, Susan, 20, 25
Modernism, 29
Mohanty, Satya, 13
   "The Epistemic Status of Cultural Identity," 34–35
Muckelbauer, John, 18
   Future of Invention, The, 99, 108–11
Multiplicities, 42
Murray, Donald, 84

Neel, Jasper, 47–48
Novelty, 76–78, 107

Ortmeier-Hooper, Christina, 62
Other, The, 36
Outside. *See* Exteriority

Pedersen, Anne-Marie, 60
Performativity, of identity, 16, 57–58, 66
Pike, Kenneth, 105
Postmodernism
   and composition studies, 23–26
   and exteriority, 23
   and technology, 29
Poststructuralism, and identity, 9–10
Prior, Paul
   on inscription vs. composition, 3
   on writing process, 1
   on writing's origins, 10–11

Proairetic codes, 83–85
Punctum, 5–6

Readings, Bill, 12
Reid, Alexander, *The Two Virtuals: New Media and Composition*, 41–43
Relationality
   and ecological model of invention, 82
   of writing, 3, 85, 90
Remixes. *See* Iterability, defined
Richards, I. A., 58
Rickert, Thomas, *Ambient Rhetoric*, 91–96
Rorty, Richard, 36

Sánchez, Raúl, *The Function of Theory in Composition Studies*, 2
Schilb, John, 19
Schwartz, Gwen Gray, 62
Shuck, Gail, 60
Signified, 8
Signifiers, 4–6
Spivak, Gayatri, 27
Strategic essentialism, 27
Studium, 6
Style
   and interiority, 98–99
   and invention, 100, 104–7
   and novelty, 107
   theories of, 18, 99–103
Subjects, vs. writers, 20–22

Technology
   materiality of, 29–30
   modernist vs. postmodernist views of, 29
Terminology
   of exteriority, 9
   influence of, 7–8
   of materiality, 30
Terranova, Tiziana, 49–50
Textuality
   concept of, 20
   transparency of, 21–22

Ulmer, Gregory, 26, 87, 90, 94–95
Ultimate terms, 30

"Virtual-actual" concept, 42
Vital empirics, 86–91
Vitanza, Victor, 35, 89

Wegner, Phillip, 12
Weisser, Christian, 59
Williams, Bronwyn T., 62
Worsham, Lynn, 60
Writers
   agency of, 10, 14, 79–80
   and authorship, 43–45
   embodiment of, 16, 63–65
   vs. subjects, 20–22
Writing
   as circulation, 52–56
   as communication, 46–48
   as event, 12–13
   exteriority of, 7–9
   as information, 48–52
   relationality of, 3, 85, 90
   as technology of representation, 2–3

Yagelski, Robert P., 76

AUTHOR

Raúl Sánchez is associate professor of English at the University of Florida, where he teaches courses in advanced composition, technical writing, composition theory, rhetorical theory, critical theory, cultural studies, and postcolonial theory. He is the author of *The Function of Theory in Composition Studies* (2005) and the coeditor (with Iris D. Ruiz) of *Decolonizing Rhetoric and Composition Studies: New Latinx Keywords for Theory and Pedagogy* (2016). He is a former co-chair of the Latinx Caucus of NCTE/CCCC and has been a member of that caucus since 1994.

BOOKS IN THE CCCC STUDIES IN WRITING & RHETORIC SERIES

Inside the Subject: A Theory of Identity for the Study of Writing
Raúl Sánchez

Genre of Power: Police Report Writers and Readers in the Justice System
Leslie Seawright

Assembling Composition
Edited by Kathleen Blake Yancey and Stephen J. McElroy

Public Pedagogy in Composition Studies
Ashley J. Holmes

From Boys to Men: Rhetorics of Emergent American Masculinity
Leigh Ann Jones

Freedom Writing: African American Civil Rights Literacy Activism, 1955–1967
Rhea Estelle Lathan

The Desire for Literacy: Writing in the Lives of Adult Learners
Lauren Rosenberg

On Multimodality: New Media in Composition Studies
Jonathan Alexander and Jacqueline Rhodes

Toward a New Rhetoric of Difference
Stephanie L. Kerschbaum

Rhetoric of Respect: Recognizing Change at a Community Writing Center
Tiffany Rousculp

After Pedagogy: The Experience of Teaching
Paul Lynch

Redesigning Composition for Multilingual Realities
Jay Jordan

Agency in the Age of Peer Production
Quentin D. Vieregge, Kyle D. Stedman, Taylor Joy Mitchell, and Joseph M. Moxley

Remixing Composition: A History of Multimodal Writing Pedagogy
Jason Palmeri

First Semester: Graduate Students, Teaching Writing, and the Challenge of Middle Ground
Jessica Restaino

Agents of Integration: Understanding Transfer as a Rhetorical Act
Rebecca S. Nowacek

Digital Griots: African American Rhetoric in a Multimedia Age
Adam J. Banks

The Managerial Unconscious in the History of Composition Studies
Donna Strickland

Everyday Genres: Writing Assignments across the Disciplines
Mary Soliday

The Community College Writer: Exceeding Expectations
Howard Tinberg and Jean-Paul Nadeau

A Taste for Language: Literacy, Class, and English Studies
James Ray Watkins

Before Shaughnessy: Basic Writing at Yale and Harvard, 1920–1960
Kelly Ritter

Writer's Block: The Cognitive Dimension
Mike Rose

Teaching/Writing in Thirdspaces: The Studio Approach
Rhonda C. Grego and Nancy S. Thompson

Rural Literacies
Kim Donehower, Charlotte Hogg, and Eileen E. Schell

Writing with Authority: Students' Roles as Writers in Cross-National Perspective
David Foster

Whistlin' and Crowin' Women of Appalachia: Literacy Practices since College
Katherine Kelleher Sohn

Sexuality and the Politics of Ethos in the Writing Classroom
Zan Meyer Gonçalves

African American Literacies Unleashed: Vernacular English and the Composition Classroom
Arnetha F. Ball and Ted Lardner

Revisionary Rhetoric, Feminist Pedagogy, and Multigenre Texts
Julie Jung

Archives of Instruction: Nineteenth-Century Rhetorics, Readers, and Composition Books in the United States
Jean Ferguson Carr, Stephen L. Carr, and Lucille M. Schultz

Response to Reform: Composition and the Professionalization of Teaching
Margaret J. Marshall

Multiliteracies for a Digital Age
Stuart A. Selber

Personally Speaking: Experience as Evidence in Academic Discourse
Candace Spigelman

Self-Development and College Writing
Nick Tingle

Minor Re/Visions: Asian American Literacy Narratives as a Rhetoric of Citizenship
Morris Young

A Communion of Friendship: Literacy, Spiritual Practice, and Women in Recovery
Beth Daniell

Embodied Literacies: Imageword and a Poetics of Teaching
Kristie S. Fleckenstein

Language Diversity in the Classroom: From Intention to Practice
Edited by Geneva Smitherman and Victor Villanueva

Rehearsing New Roles: How College Students Develop as Writers
Lee Ann Carroll

Across Property Lines: Textual Ownership in Writing Groups
Candace Spigelman

Mutuality in the Rhetoric and Composition Classroom
David L. Wallace and Helen Rothschild Ewald

The Young Composers: Composition's Beginnings in Nineteenth-Century Schools
Lucille M. Schultz

Technology and Literacy in the Twenty-First Century: The Importance of Paying Attention
Cynthia L. Selfe

Women Writing the Academy: Audience, Authority, and Transformation
Gesa E. Kirsch

Gender Influences: Reading Student Texts
Donnalee Rubin

Something Old, Something New: College Writing Teachers and Classroom Change
Wendy Bishop

Dialogue, Dialectic, and Conversation: A Social Perspective on the Function of Writing
Gregory Clark

Audience Expectations and Teacher Demands
Robert Brooke and John Hendricks

Toward a Grammar of Passages
Richard M. Coe

Rhetoric and Reality: Writing Instruction in American Colleges, 1900–1985
James A. Berlin

Writing Groups: History, Theory, and Implications
Anne Ruggles Gere

Teaching Writing as a Second Language
Alice S. Horning

Invention as a Social Act
Karen Burke LeFevre

The Variables of Composition: Process and Product in a Business Setting
Glenn J. Broadhead and Richard C. Freed

Writing Instruction in Nineteenth-Century American Colleges
James A. Berlin

Computers & Composing: How the New Technologies Are Changing Writing
Jeanne W. Halpern and Sarah Liggett

A New Perspective on Cohesion in Expository Paragraphs
Robin Bell Markels

Evaluating College Writing Programs
Stephen P. Witte and Lester Faigley

This book was typeset in Garamond and Frutiger by Barbara Frazier.
Typefaces used on the cover include Adobe Garamond and Formata.
The book was printed on 55-lb. Natural Offset paper
by King Printing Company, Inc.

www.ingramcontent.com/pod-product-compliance
Lightning Source LLC
Chambersburg PA
CBHW061957220426
43662CB00011B/1729